Foucault and Neoliberalism

Foucault and Neoliberalism

Edited by

Daniel Zamora and Michael C. Behrent

polity

First published in French as *Critiquer Foucault: Les années 1980 et la tentation néolibérale* © Les Éditions Aden, 2014
Reprinted 2016 (three times), 2017 (twice), 2020, 2021

This collection © Polity Press 2016
Introduction & Chapter 3 copyright © Daniel Zamora
Chapters 1 & 8 copyright © Michael Scott Christofferson
Chapter 2 copyright © Cambridge University Press
Chapter 4 copyright © Mitchell Dean
Chapter 5 copyright © Loïc Wacquant
Chapter 6 copyright © Koninklijk Brill NV
Chapter 7 copyright © Jean-Loup Amselle
Conclusion copyright © Michael C. Behrent

Polity Press
65 Bridge Street
Cambridge CB2 1UR, UK

Polity Press
350 Main Street
Malden, MA 02148, USA

ISBN-13: 978-1-5095-0176-2
ISBN-13: 978-1-5095-0177-9 (pb)

A catalog record for this book is available from the British Library.

Library of Congress Cataloging-in-Publication Data

Zamora, Daniel (Doctoral Candidate)
    Foucault and neoliberalism / Daniel Zamora, Michael C. Behrent.
        pages cm
    Includes bibliographical references and index.
    ISBN 978-1-5095-0176-2 (hardback : alk. paper) – ISBN 978-1-5095-0177-9 (paperback : alk. paper)   1. Foucault, Michel, 1926-1984.   2. Neoliberalism.   I. Title.
    B2430.F724Z36 2015
    194–dc23
                              2015013023

Typeset in 10.5 on 12 pt Sabon
by Toppan Best-set Premedia Limited
Printed and bound in the United States by LSC Communications

The publisher has used its best endeavors to ensure that the URLs for external websites referred to in this book are correct and active at the time of going to press. However, the publisher has no responsibility for the websites and can make no guarantee that a site will remain live or that the content is or will remain appropriate.

Every effort has been made to trace all copyright holders, but if any have been inadvertently overlooked the publisher will be pleased to include any necessary credits in any subsequent reprint or edition.

For further information on Polity, visit our website:
politybooks.com

Contents

Contributors

Jean-Loup Amselle is Professor of Anthropology at l'École des hautes études en sciences sociales (EHESS) in Paris. He is the Director of the *Cahiers d'Études Africaines* and is the author of *Affirmative Exclusion: Cultural Pluralism and the Rule of Custom in France* (Cornell, 2003).

Michael C. Behrent is an American historian who teaches modern French history and European intellectual history at Appalachian State University in North Carolina. He is currently preparing a book on the work of Michel Foucault during the 1970s and the neoliberal turn in French thought.

Michael Scott Christofferson is Associate Professor of History at Adelphi University, New York. Since completing a Ph.D. supervised by Robert Paxton, he has published *French Intellectuals against the Left: The Antitotalitarian Moment of the 1970s* (2004), and he is currently finishing a critical biography of François Furet.

Mitchell Dean is Professor of Public Governance at the Copenhagen Business School. While a dedicated Foucauldian for many years, he has come to question whether a Foucauldian problematic of power and politics is sufficient for present issues. This concern is reflected in his recent book *The Signature of Power: Sovereignty, Governmentality and Biopolitics* (2013).

Jan Rehmann is Visiting Professor of Critical Theory and Social Analysis at the Union Theological Seminary in New York. He also teaches philosophy at the Free University of Berlin. He is co-editor of the journal *Das Argument* and of the *Historical-Critical Dictionary of Marxism* (HKWM). He has published (among other titles) *Max Weber: Modernization as Passive Revolution. A Gramscian Analysis* (2015), *Theories of Ideology: The Powers of Alienation and Subjection* (2014), *Pedagogy of the Poor* (2011, with Willie Baptist), and *Postmodernist Neo-Nietzscheanism* (2004).

Loïc Wacquant is Professor of Sociology at the University of California, Berkeley, and a researcher at the Centre de sociologie européenne, Paris. His work spans urban relegation, ethnoracial domination, the penal state, incarnation, and social theory and the politics of reason. His books have been translated into 20 languages and include *Body and Soul: Notebooks of an Apprentice Boxer* (2004; new expanded edition, 2015), *The Two Faces of the Poor* (2015), and *Tracking the Penal State* (2016). For more information, see loicwacquant.net

Daniel Zamora is a sociologist at the Université Libre de Bruxelles (ULB) specializing in welfare policies under neoliberalism. His current work concerns the history of unemployment and poverty in Europe since the 1970s.

Acknowledgements

The contributions to this book originally appeared in French as *Critiquer Foucault. Les années 1980 et la tentation néo-libérale*, with some exceptions:

Portions of chapter 1 were originally published in: Michael Scott Christofferson, *French Intellectuals against the Left: The Antitotalitarian Moment of the 1970s* (New York: Berghahn Books, 2004). Reproduced with permission.

Chapter 2 was originally published as: Michael C. Behrent, "Liberalism without Humanism: Michel Foucault and the Free-market Creed, 1976–1979," *Modern Intellectual History*, Volume 6(3), pp. 539–68 (2009) © Cambridge University Press. Reproduced with permission.

Chapter 4 is a new contribution to the English edition. Portions were originally published as: Mitchell Dean, "Michel Foucault's 'Apology' for Neoliberalism," *Journal of Political Power*, Volume 7(3), pp. 433–42.

Portions of chapter 6 were originally published in: Jan Rehmann, *Theories of Ideology: The Powers of Alienation and Subjection* (Leiden: Koninklijk Brill NV, 2013). Reproduced with permission.

Introduction

Foucault, the Left, and the 1980s

Daniel Zamora

In an interview with Paul Rabinow, Michel Foucault observed, in 1984, shortly before his death:

> I think I have in fact been situated in most of the squares on the political checkerboard, one after another and sometimes simultaneously: as anarchist, leftist, ostentatious or disguised Marxist, nihilist or secret anti-Marxist, technocrat in the service of Gaullism, new liberal, etc. ... None of these descriptions is important by itself; taken together, on the other hand, they mean something. And I must admit I rather like what they mean.[1]

This wide array of labels, which are as contradictory as they are unsuited for describing this giant of twentieth-century French thought, are nevertheless consistent with his reputation. In his rich body of work, and through his ability to conceptualize and even anticipate the central questions of his time, Foucault always seemed able to interrogate major contemporary issues in exciting and innovative ways. As a member of the French Communist Party, during his Gaullist phase, and even when he gravitated toward Maoism, he always remained critical of the movements to which he adhered. As a "fellow traveler" in a period that he shook up, intellectually speaking, Foucault always seemed one step ahead of his contemporaries. This is why the wide variety of receptions and readings his work has received is understandable. As the outcome of the varied and contradictory schools of thought that influenced him, his work cannot, fundamentally, be reduced to a single label.

After Foucault's death in 1984, Paul Veyne went as far as saying that his work marked "the most important event of thought of our century." Thirty years after his death, it is clear that he has well and truly become one of the most influential thinkers of the last 40 years, both in French intellectual life and abroad. His work is widely disseminated, translated, and taught around the world, well beyond educational institutions. His ideas, moreover, have been used in fields as diverse as history, philosophy, anthropology, political science, and sociology. His work has greatly inspired many contemporary thinkers in the fields of gender studies, postcolonial studies, and what is more generally known as postmodernism. His influence on intellectual life is vast and has significantly shaped the terms of intellectual debates of the second half of the twentieth century. Foucault has, for better or worse, become a central intellectual reference of our time.

This intellectual hegemony is particularly pronounced in the realm of academic critical theory. He has acquired an almost saint-like stature, as much for his work as for his conception of intellectual engagement, which he embodied in his many political battles. At present, there is no longer any university or group of critical reflection that has not, directly or indirectly, been affected in some way by Foucault's work.

This association of the man who gave us the "specific intellectual" with the contemporary critical Left should nevertheless be examined in the light of his positions and the movements with which he was associated in the final decade of his life. Indeed, if his Maoist period or his brief membership in the Communist Party are relatively uncontroversial among his leftist disciples, the same cannot be said of his later commitments.

Whether it be his support of the "new philosophers," his analysis of governmentality, or his ambiguous relationship to neoliberalism in the late 1970s and early 1980s, these later positions make many Foucault scholars uneasy. Indeed, Foucault did not content himself merely with questioning certain aspects of neoliberal thought: he seems, rather, to have been seduced by some of its key ideas. These issues, far from simply embodying the development of an intellectual, illustrate more generally some of the shifts that occurred in the Left post-1968, its disillusionment, and a profound transformation of the French intellectual field.

The 1980s were, after all, a decade of renunciation: first on the part of the Socialist government (as it largely abandoned the program on which it rode to power), then of intellectuals. François Mitterrand's 1981 victory paved the way for many a disappointment and failure, particularly the abandonment of the project of "transforming the world" for that of accommodating neoliberalism. Yesterday's fellow travelers became neoliberalism's facilitators and passionate opponents of any attempt to transform society. All they had once celebrated was now seen as part of a problematic that inevitably led to the "totalitarian temptation." In this way, the state, social security, redistribution, public property, and nationalization came to be seen as outdated and conservative ideas.

How should we interpret Foucault's radical position on social security, which he essentially saw as the culmination of "biopower?" Or his support – stronger than we would like to think – of the "new philosophers"? How should we view his lectures on *The Birth of Biopolitics* and his presumed sympathy for the emerging and very social-liberal "Second Left"? One might, finally, question his illusory belief that neoliberal forms of power would be less disciplinary and that prisons would ultimately disappear. These questions pertain not only to Foucault himself, but also to the ambiguities inherent in the Left (or at least a part of it), and especially some of its intellectual spokespersons, in light of neoliberalism's rising tide.

Whether on the question of the State, social security, "care of the self," prison, autonomy, or power, it is clear that criticisms traditionally made by the "libertarian" Left have been profoundly destabilized in the wake of the neoliberal offensive. Indeed, far from opposing these key libertarian ideas, the neoliberal movement, on the contrary, mobilized them in the (largely successful) symbolic *coup d'état* that it has launched against the defenders of the welfare state. The conception of social security as a system of "social control" and the Left's defense of individual autonomy during the "Thirty Glorious Years" of postwar growth, in opposition to the worker's alienation in the capitalist system of mass production, was recycled into a critique of the state and its "bureaucracy." More generally, the freedom of individuals was celebrated, over and against the social structures which enslaved them, in what became a general critique of the state, unions, parties, the family, and all other intermediate structures that were being undermined to make way for neoliberal policies.

This intellectual recycling, which is the heart of capitalism's "new spirit," should lead us to question retroactively the theoretical moves made by a number of leading left-wing intellectuals in the late 1960s, particularly the often astonishing trajectories of former Maoists who converted so suddenly to the dogma of the market economy. We should also ask whether this "conversion" is even all that surprising.

Did their opposition to all that the "old" Left and its institutions embodied not foreshadow their subsequent "betrayal"? This question, while perhaps provocative, is no less legitimate and stimulating. Understanding the 1980s and the triumph of neoliberalism requires an exploration of the most ambiguous redoubts of the intellectual Left during this period, and not least one of its most important figures. Many recent studies return to this period. Some see Foucault as enamored of neoliberalism,[2] while others have maintained that he was critical of it and, more recently, have argued that he used neoliberalism to question social theory.[3] These very different (and even contradictory) readings are reflective of the ambiguities and tensions that have troubled the Left since 1968.

While it is impossible to know what path Foucault would have taken, it is nevertheless interesting to consider several episodes that show some of his lesser-known views. While the renunciation and "conversion" to neoliberalism of key figures of the intellectual Left is often emphasized, relatively little is said about how certain developments in Foucault's later work, which would seem to be beyond reproach, paradoxically functioned to legitimate a neoliberal common sense. Though they are frequently overlooked or dismissed by his supporters as "details" or "misunderstandings" of the author's real intentions, the ambiguities they reveal raise very stimulating questions about the period.

The purpose of this book is thus to examine Michel Foucault's work and commitments during his final years through various lenses – yet ones that nonetheless capture the key debates of the period, in which a Left that was victorious at the polls saw its intellectual foundations seriously weakened. Our intention is thus not to attempt to answer the wrong question: namely, whether Foucault became neoliberal at the end of his life. As an alternative to this question, which is sterile and limits the debate to very narrow considerations, we will consider a range of questions. It is not a matter of being "for" or "against" Foucault, but rather of discussing, engaging with, and critiquing him to better grasp the extent of his influence and the issues he opened up in the intellectual field.

This book thus seeks to open historical and theoretical inroads at junctures where it seemed stimulating to interrogate the choices and thinking of this superstar of twentieth-century French thought – not only to better understand a moment in time, but also to question our own assumptions about what a critical theory must be.

Notes

1 M. Foucault, "Polemics, Politics, and Problematizations," trans. Lydia Davis, in *The Foucault Reader*, ed. P. Rabinow (New York: Pantheon Books, 1984), 383–4.
2 See, notably, J. L. Moreno Pestaña, *Foucault, la gauche et la politique* (Paris: Textuel, 2011).
3 See G. de Lagasnerie, *La dernière leçon de Michel Foucault* (Paris: Fayard, 2012).

1

Foucault and New Philosophy: Why Foucault Endorsed André Glucksmann's *The Master Thinkers**

Michael Scott Christofferson

In 1977, "new philosophy" took French intellectual and political life by storm. In their runaway best-selling books, "new philosophers," the most notable of whom were André Glucksmann and Bernard Henri Lévy, offered a radical critique of Marxism and revolutionary politics by linking them both to the Gulag. Further, they argued that transformative politics in general and, at the limit, reason and science were dangerously affiliated with totalitarianism. The only safe politics, they suggested, was the defense of human rights. This was a crucial moment in French intellectual and political life that marked the end of the revolutionary upsurge begun by 1968 and the transition to more moderate liberal and republican political options. Making sense of it is crucial for understanding both recent French history and, more specifically, the trajectories of the intellectuals engaged in it. This is notably the case for Michel Foucault, a central figure in the ideological–political debates of the 1970s.

Foucault intervened in the debate over new philosophy with a laudatory review of Glucksmann's *The Master Thinkers* in the May 9–15, 1977 issue of the mass-circulation weekly *Le Nouvel Observateur*. Foucault's intervention was important for himself, for Glucksmann, and for "new philosophy" in general. For Foucault, it was not a minor matter. His support for Glucksmann resulted in irreparable breaks with old friends, such as Claude Mauriac and, most notably, Gilles Deleuze, who had broadly shared Foucault's Nietzchean inspiration and post-1968 philosophical and political trajectory, but was sharply critical of new philosophy and remained, unlike Foucault, more generally supportive of post-1968 radicalism.[1] For Glucksmann and new philosophy, Foucault's endorsement was even more important because, as I have argued elsewhere,[2] new philosophy, although a mass-media phenomenon, would have been much less successful if it had not received support from leading intellectuals.

Foucault's praise for *The Master Thinkers* has presented something of a mystery to scholars of Foucault because Glucksmann arguably simplified and twisted Foucault's ideas beyond recognition. Evaluations of it have consequently differed greatly. Didier Eribon, Foucault's first biographer, downplays its importance by holding that Foucault's support for *The Master Thinkers* was "dictated more by political than by philosophical considerations."[3] By contrast, Michael C. Behrent argues in his contribution to this volume that "the extent to which this shift [the anti-totalitarian one in new philosophy] impacted his own thinking has been underestimated" (p. 26). Here I will address the problem of Foucault's support for Glucksmann as a point of departure for understanding Foucault's politics and conception of power in the early to mid-1970s. While complicating Eribon's picture of Foucault taking a primarily political position, I also seek to demonstrate that Foucault's endorsement of Glucksmann was hardly accidental, but rather a reflection of Foucault's philosophical practice, its relationship with politics and the mass media, and shortcomings in his conception of power that limited its effectiveness for thinking about the twentieth century. It may be from Behrent's downstream perspective that the moment of new philosophy was a turning point for Foucault, but looking upstream toward 1977 Foucault's endorsement of Glucksmann was less of a break with Foucault's past than it may seem.

André Glucksmann's *The Master Thinkers* was the culmination of Glucksmann's disaffection with post-1968 revolutionary politics and his effort to turn a broader public away from it and other efforts at radical political transformation such as that represented by the Union of the Left, which seemed likely to win the March 1978 legislative elections when Glucksmann's book was published in 1977. Glucksmann, who had been a member of the Maoist *Gauche prolétarienne* in the early 1970s, had already tried to justify and explain his disillusionment with the revolutionary Left in his 1975 book *La cuisinière et le mangeur d'hommes: essai sur l'État, le marxisme, et les camps de concentration* [*The Cook and the Cannibal: Essay on the State, Marxism, and the Concentration Camps*]. Taking as his point of departure Solzhenitsyn's *The Gulag Archipelago* and the French response to it, Glucksmann argues that the Gulag is a culminating point of Western historical development, the great moments of which are "Platonism (and its slaves), classical Reason (and its inmates), Marxism (and its camps)."[4] The Gulag and its Marxist theoretical foundation are but the latest effort by elites to build up state structures and ideologies to dominate the masses, which Glucksmann calls "the pleb." This link between the Gulag and the West explains, Glucksmann argues, why French intellectuals have not been more indignant in the face of the Gulag. Considering theory and the state to be instruments of domination, Glucksmann calls for a politics of resistance by the pleb in both East and West. These populist and anarchist conclusions find sustenance in Foucault's work. Foucault's *Madness and Civilization: A History of Insanity in the Age of Reason* (1961) is used by Glucksmann to establish the link between Western historical development and the Gulag, as it was in his view "the general hospital," "crowning achievement of the new Reason," that "prefigures the concentration camp."[5] For Glucksmann, the twentieth century "innovates little" in relation to this earlier precedent, "even the idea *of deporting* is not its own; the general hospital already served as the warehouse for the unfortunate that one rounded up [*raflait*] to send them 'to the Islands'."[6] Foucault was central not only to Glucksmann's historical analysis, but also to his political response to it. Politics, Glucksmann stated in 1975, should take a Foucauldian turn, focusing its aim on micropowers, the disciplines that are at "the root of the state power."[7]

Glucksmann's *The Master Thinkers* of 1977 follows the same line of argumentation as his earlier *The Cook and the Cannibal*. Joining Marx in infamy are Hegel, Fichte, and

Nietzsche, also presented by Glucksmann as philosophers of a coercive and normalizing state. Glucksmann argues that these "master thinkers" systematized and justified the modern state's project of domination, itself put on the "order of the day" by the French Revolution. They promoted an interiorization of the law that smothers the pleb's protest at its inception. While not directly responsible for the Gulag and Auschwitz, they "systematized and rendered strategically malleable ideas and tactics largely diffused before them in societies in the process of becoming rationally disciplinary." They are guilty for having "under the cover of knowledge ...put together the mental apparatus indispensable to the launching of the great final solutions of the twentieth century."[8]

Glucksmann's book is constructed around a number of homologous oppositions: the state versus the pleb, anti-Semitism versus Judaism, revolution and power versus resistance, and reason and science versus ignorance. The state seeks to dominate the pleb, submit it to its will and force it to internalize its subordination. This project leads directly to anti-Semitism, the camps, and genocide:

> *All that wanders*, that is the question. Under the cloak of the Jew one condemns an entire little world that threatens to elude the state in crossing frontiers, and that, in transgressing them, upsets disciplinary society. The Europe of states seeks to exclude the marginal. The master thinkers step down for the master purgers who mix Jews and homosexuals in the Nazi camps and all that deviates in the Russian camps. Liberal Europe wanted to assimilate and normalize more calmly; cultural genocide substitutes for physical genocide.

Although the project of domination is that of the state, intellectuals, science, and reason are all essentially complicit in it. Science and the texts of the master thinkers are simply strategies of domination, and "to think is to dominate." Conversely, behind Nazism and Stalinism lie texts and science. Neither of them is a phenomenon circumscribed to a particular time or place: they are located in the texts that form the cultural heritage of Europe. Sociological explanations of socialist regimes are, like explanations of Nazism by German

militarism, illegitimate and interested efforts to divert attention from that which is essential to them: the European state's
project of domination systematized in the texts of the master
thinkers. Revolution is not an option; it does not lead to
fundamental change. Mirroring what already exists and con-
veyed by a science of revolution, it is above all the project of
the state to increase its domination. Embracing anti-
intellectualism, Glucksmann praises the merits of ignorance.
Identifying reason and revolution with domination, he lauds
the authenticity of unreflective self-interested action: the resistance of the pleb and the panurgic "Do what thou wilt" ["*Fay
ce que vouldras*"].[9]

As it did in *The Cook and the Cannibal*, Foucault's work
plays a key role in *The Master Thinkers*, except this time
Glucksmann's main reference is to Foucault's *Discipline and
Punish: The Birth of the Prison* (1975). The master thinkers
were exploring "a new solidarity of knowledge and power,
of experts and disciplinary society." Their dream was to fab-
ricate subjects who had internalized discipline so as to achieve
"a prison without wardens," the ultimate manifestation of
the panoptic ideal that Foucault analyzed in *Discipline and
Punish* and that was, according to Glucksmann, central to
Hegel's idea of the State. Although the multiple references
to panopticism and the disciplinary society were sufficient to
make clear Glucksmann's debt to Foucault, Glucksmann
stated his admiration for Foucault openly by calling him the
first since Marx to systematically interrogate "the most
immediate origins of the modern world."[10]

Foucault's review of *The Master Thinkers* accepted Glucksmann's basic premise that the "great rage of facts" now justifies suspicion of grand theories. Following Glucksmann, he
accepted the need to confront philosophy with the horrors of
the twentieth century, to "plaster onto ideas the death's-heads
that resemble them." It was, Foucault stated in apparent
agreement with Glucksmann, the master thinkers' vision of
"the state-revolution with all its final solutions" that lay at
the foundation of all of the systems of domination and massacres of the twentieth century. The review issued no criticism
and indicated no point of divergence between Foucault and
Glucksmann. Further, later that year, in a discussion of
abusive rapprochements of the Western "confinement" he

had analyzed in *Madness and Civilization* and the Gulag, Foucault stated that "Glucksmann's analysis avoids all these superpositions [*rabattements*] that are so readily done."[11]

Foucault's consistent support of Glucksmann is all the more striking considering that Glucksmann's ideas, notably his conceptions of power and reason, were, as Peter Dews has argued in an article on the question, foreign to the more rigorous analyses of Foucault. Glucksmann identified power with the state and postulated the existence of a pleb that largely escapes both, whereas Foucault, at his most innovative, considered power to be diffuse and analyzed it in terms of micro-structures that he explicitly developed in opposition to a conceptualization of power in terms of sovereignty located in the state. Less subtle than Foucault, Glucksmann only recognized a more complicated idea of power when he could use it to draw anti-revolutionary conclusions: "Everyone participates in the reproduction of exploitation... Taking into account this internal division should make it impossible to imagine a single, ultimate revolution confronting the good against the bad in a decisive battle. If nobody completely escapes the reproduction of relations of exploitation; if everyone is *double*, the greatest number will find themselves at the end of their own rifle."[12] Further, Glucksmann's complete identification of Reason (understood by him as a philosophical and Hegelian Reason) and science with domination is alien to Foucault's genealogies, which seek to explain the emergence of particular forms of reason and science "at the point of articulation of discursive and non-discursive practices." In Foucault's analysis of the great confinement, for example, "Reason" itself is not culpable.[13]

Part of the explanation for Foucault's endorsement of Glucksmann lies in Foucault's use of the mass media in his strategy of intellectual consecration. Foucault had, in the 1960s, converted his academic credentials into cultural celebrity by increasing his visibility in intellectual reviews and the cultural press, eventually achieving intellectual superstardom with the publication of *The Order of Things: An Archaeology of the Human Sciences*, which was extensively discussed in the mass media and became a bestseller in the summer of 1966. This cultural celebrity was, in turn, an important factor contributing to Foucault's election to the Collège de France in 1970. In the 1970s, Foucault continued to thirst for recognition in the broader intellectual scene and wrote books that were eminently relevant to contemporary issues. Although Glucksmann may have distorted Foucault's ideas, he was a useful ally in Foucault's bid for recognition – especially after Foucault's disappointment with the reception of *The Will to Knowledge*, volume I of his *History of Sexuality*, in 1976. Glucksmann praised Foucault to the sky in books that sold in large numbers and were well promoted in the media. Although it might have been more principled for Foucault to criticize Glucksmann's simplifications, it would have been both rude and self-defeating for him not to return the favor by complimenting Glucksmann.

An examination of Foucault's philosophical practice and its relationship to politics shed additional light on Foucault's endorsement of Glucksmann. The contrast with Deleuze in this regard is particularly interesting. As Judith Revel told François Dosse, "Foucault starts with experiences and practices and then conceptualizes. Deleuze and Guattari invent war machines and try them out."[14] Foucault never stood still, was constantly evolving, and took positions that his philosophy could not justify – yet, if ever. Further – and perhaps this reflects less favorably on him – Foucault had a history of taking philosophico-political stances that seem to be based more on a desire to situate himself within the intellectual avant-garde than on sincere conviction. A good example of this is his Marxist stance in the early 1970s. Foucault had thoroughly rejected Marxist analysis before 1968 and had so little interest in Marxist debates that "the words 'capitalist' and 'proletariat' do not appear in *any* work by Foucault prior to 1970."[15] Foucault would never become a Marxist, yet having recognized Marxism's power as a Sorelian myth while in Tunisia in 1968, he made what might be called a strategic alliance with it. Beginning in 1969, Marxist references began to enter his vocabulary. When given the opportunity to recruit the philosophy department at the experimental university of Vincennes, Foucault appointed Marxists, even offering a position to André Glucksmann, who turned it down.[16] This Marxist turn did not last long, reaching its high point in 1972 and declining thereafter, until Foucault began explicitly rejecting Marxism in 1975–6. While Foucault's adoption of a

Marxist vocabulary was not entirely insincere, insofar as it expressed Foucault's sympathy for the period's revolutionary Left, his *marxisant* pronouncements would have been hard for him to justify philosophically, and he never really tried to do so. The same might be said of his endorsement of Glucksmann in 1977. At this point, Foucault wished to support the general political position represented by Glucksmann, and the consistency of his endorsement with his philosophy was not something that seems to have been of great concern to him. Deleuze, more the pure philosopher in this case, could not, by contrast, stomach Glucksmann's simplifications and, moreover, disagreeing with him politically, found Foucault's endorsement unacceptable.[17]

Much of the motivation for Foucault's support of Glucksmann was political and must be understood in relationship to his anti-statist attachment to direct democracy, his vehement anti-communism, and his criticism of the Union of the Left. Foucault's politics in the early 1970s were infused with direct-democratic populism, as can be seen in his work in the Groupe d'information sur les prisons (GIP) and his reformulation of the role of the intellectual. After the imprisonment of leftist militants brought new attention to prison conditions, Foucault founded the GIP in February 1971. Although it was originally affiliated with the Maoist Gauche prolétarienne, Foucault gave it an original direction. Rejecting claims to representation or authority, the GIP refused to formulate a plan to reform prison conditions and asserted that its sole goal was to allow prisoners to express themselves and make known the reality of prison conditions so that they might themselves drive the agenda for change. Its motto was "Let the prisoners talk!" [*La parole aux détenus!*]. This same aversion to representation and hierarchy can be seen in the idea of the "specific intellectual" formulated by Foucault and Deleuze in 1972. Rejecting representation in general, Foucault also rejected the traditional intellectual, defined by him as someone who "said the truth to those who did not yet see it and in the name of those who could not say it." The traditional intellectual is part of a system of power that forbids the "discourse" and the "knowledge" of the masses. The "specific intellectual," by contrast, should not place himself outside of the masses "to tell the mute truth of everyone" but fight with the masses and specifically "against the forms of power of which he is at the same time the object and the instrument: in the order of 'knowledge,' of 'truth,' of 'consciousness' and of 'discourse.'" What counts is the "counter-discourse" of the prisoners or delinquents and not a discourse or theory of delinquency. The masses do not need the intellectuals in order to think; indeed, "they know perfectly, clearly, much better than them [the intellectuals], and they say it very well." As Foucault would later put it, "the knowledge of an intellectual is always incomplete in relation to worker knowledge." Intellectuals should simply be facilitators of popular self-expression.[18]

The distance between these positions and Glucksmann's celebration of popular resistance against the philosophical systems of the "master thinkers" is not great, especially as Foucault shared with Glucksmann the concept of the "pleb." Indeed, Foucault first uses the term in 1972 in a dialogue on popular justice with Glucksmann and other members of the Gauche prolétarienne. Here, Foucault refers to the "non-proletarianized pleb" as an implicit alternative to the Marxist term "lumpenproletariat," which was similar to the latter in being déclassé, but rather different in that Foucault considered it to be the agent of revolution.[19] In late 1977, Foucault spoke of this formerly revolutionary pleb in terms reminiscent of the pleb that defies power in Glucksmann's *The Master Thinkers*. Here Foucault stated that the pleb was not a sociological category but one defined by the fact that "there is always something in the social body, in classes, in groups, in individuals themselves that in a certain way escapes relations of power." "'The' pleb," Foucault explained, "undoubtedly does not exist, but there is 'some' pleb" in all individuals, insofar as they "respond to all advances of power by a movement to disengage from it."[20]

Beyond these theoretical discussions of power and resistance to it, Foucault and Glucksmann found common political ground in the mid-1970s in their anti-communism and antipathy toward the Union of the Left. As I have argued at length in *French Intellectuals against the Left*, the Union of the Left and, behind it, the French Communist Party (Parti Communiste Français; PCF) worried many French intellectuals. There was no love lost between the Communist Party and intellectuals, and much of the latter's rethinking of the revolutionary project of the 1960s and 1970s was explicitly formulated as an alternative to the Soviet model and Leninist politics, which were seen as failures. Glucksmann and Foucault, both of whom had been in the French Communist Party in their youth, hated the PCF. For them and many others the 1970s Union of the Left alliance between the Socialist Party and PCF threatened to revive and bring to power the old forms of state socialism that they had long ago rejected. The problem became urgent in 1977 because the Union's growing electoral success in the mid-1970s seemed likely to culminate in its victory in the 1978 legislative elections.

Much of Glucksmann's vitriol was directed against this alliance and the PCF within it. Indeed, his 1975 *The Cook and the Cannibal* was motivated by his disgust with what he took to be the Left's unwillingness to listen to the message of Solzhenitsyn because it did not want to "lose hope in [*désespérer*] the Common Program" – that is, the governmental program of the Union of the Left. More fundamentally – and this explains the importance he placed on the massacre-justifying theories of the master thinkers – Glucksmann believed that Marxism as a language of power prevented people from seeing clearly and made "the central committee operate in our heads."[21] Even more than *The Cook and the the Cannibal*, Glucksmann's *The Master Thinkers* was explicitly directed against the Union of the Left. It alluded to the "common program" of the "master thinkers" and called the concentration camp prisoners "those not in the program." He condemned, following Maurice Clavel's *Dieu est Dieu* [*God is God*], the politics of the "dirty handshake" [*mains sales tendues*] between the Catholic Church and the PCF, and the rallying of the clergy to the Union of the Left in the name of the liberation of man.[22] The conclusion of Glucksmann's book in the context of the political debates of 1977 was obvious: the Union of the Left was a ruse of the state and its "master thinkers" to increase their power over the pleb. Even nationalizations, Glucksmann later explained in an interview to Max Gallo, aim at the "the Jewish side of the 'private sector'...not privilege or exploitation."[23] The Left, Glucksmann implied in his book and contemporary media appearances, was dangerous because it had not reflected on the Gulag, and specifically on the role of Marxism within it.[24]

Foucault was no less violently anti-communist than Glucksmann. According to his biographer Didier Eribon, "after he quit the Communist Party and especially since he lived in Poland, Foucault developed a ferocious hatred of everything that evokes communism, directly or indirectly."[25] He blamed the poor reception of his *Madness and Civilization* of 1961, in contrast to the media-driven popular success of *The Order of Things* in 1966, on the dominance of communism and Marxism in French intellectual life. He, like many other intellectuals, used the cause of Soviet dissidence to challenge the PCF in the mid-1970s. For example, when invited onto the television program *Apostrophes* to discuss his *The Will to Knowledge* in December 1976, Foucault, incensed by the refusal of the PCF journal *La Nouvelle Critique* to publish his commentary on the trial of the Soviet Doctor Stern, used his time to discuss the trial's transcript, which had been published, with his encouragement, by Gallimard as *Un procès "ordinaire" en U.R.S.S.* [*An "Ordinary" Trial in the USSR*].

Foucault was also highly critical of the Union of the Left and did not believe that its coming to power would be of much assistance to the post-1968 social movements with which he identified. Even more, his comment that it needed to "invent an exercise of power that does not frighten people" suggests that he considered it dangerous. Asked on the eve of the 1978 legislative elections for his opinion of the Left, he responded that it was not for him to rally to the Left but for the Left to adapt to the redefinition of the political that he and others had been undertaking over the last 15 years. For this reason, Foucault was attracted by the "Second Left," those *autogestionnaire* [self-management] elements of the socialist Left who had been critical of both the Union of the Left and its Common Program. He attended the forum on social experimentation organized by it in 1977 and was sufficiently moved by Pierre Rosanvallon and Patrick Viveret's anti-totalitarian *Pour une nouvelle culture politique* [*For a New Political Culture*] to write to Rosanvallon that the book "pleased and interested me tremendously." It offered, he wrote, "a remarkable understanding of our present," "an accurate diagnosis," and "a breakthrough." It was a much needed "true," but not "immobilizing," analysis.[26]

Although Foucault's politics and use of the mass media help explain his endorsement of Glucksmann, it was ultimately ambiguities in his mid-1970s conception of power and its shortcomings in the analysis of twentieth-century communism that are most important to understanding Foucault's support for *The Master Thinkers*. In the face of these ambiguities and shortcomings, Foucault let himself be guided by his hostility to the state and other central institutions, as well as his hatred of communism. Foucault, who identified power as the issue of the twentieth century, argued that it had been fatally misunderstood because it had been posed exclusively in terms of the state and sovereignty and not in terms of disciplines – that is, configurations of power/knowledge that constituted the subject. To understand modern forms of power and to exercise some control over them, Foucault held that one had to go beyond the conceptualization of power in terms of sovereignty and the correlative understanding of power as repressive and rethink it as both diffuse – such that "we all have power in our bodies" – and productive. At this point, disciplines could be challenged by genealogies, loosely defined by Foucault as "a sort of enterprise for desubjugating historical knowledges and setting them free, that is to say capable of opposition and of struggle against the coercion of a unitary, formal, and scientific theoretical discourse."[27]

From this perspective, revolution, the desirability of which Foucault had come to question by 1977, had failed to fulfill its promises because it concentrated on the question of political sovereignty without bringing the disciplines into question. Further, it was perhaps fatally flawed because sovereign power could not, Foucault argued, limit disciplinary power. While Foucault's challenge to the repressive hypothesis (most fully developed in *The Will to Knowledge*) and assertion of the overriding importance of disciplinary power opened the door to a critique of revolution, his denial that power is shared equally allowed him to stay true to his radical direct-democratic convictions. Thus, Foucault, contrary to his radical reconceptualization of power as diffuse, continually located disciplinary power in central and institutional sites and considered resistance to it to reside in the marginal and non-institutional – which, as we have seen, he, like Glucksmann, called the pleb. Genealogies were insurrections of "knowedges...first and foremost against the effects of centralizing power that are linked to the institution and the functioning of a scientific discourse organized at the interior of a society like ours."[28] In short, the anarchistic bias of Foucault's thought led to points of convergence with Glucksmann.

The shortcomings of Foucault's analysis of twentieth-century communism are especially glaring insofar as he identified his, and more broadly his generation's, focus on the question of power as a consequence of the twentieth-century experience of fascism and Stalinism.[29] For all of Foucault's evident interest in the latter, he wrote relatively little on it, and what he wrote was often contradictory and reductive. The key issue was the relationship between disciplinary power and the use of power by the Soviet state. Here one sees continuity between his *marxisant* anarchism of the early 1970s and his analysis of disciplinary power in the middle of the decade. In 1971, Foucault saw the USSR as well as the PCF as having "taken over almost all of the value system of the bourgeoisie."[30] Further, he suggests that not only the Soviet Union's values, but also its "apparently new institutions were conceived from elements borrowed from the preceding system."[31] Later, in the mid-1970s, Foucault suggested that disciplinary power was the key element that carried over from the pre-revolutionary past and lay at the heart of exercise of power in the Soviet Union. In *Discipline and Punish*, Foucault consciously drew a direct parallel between the Gulag and the disciplining institutions of the West by describing the latter as forming a "carceral archipelago," which he intended as a reference to Solzhenitsyn.[32] On another occasion, Foucault argued that the repressive use of psychiatry in the Soviet Union followed from it having "gathered this heritage" of its use in the West. The psychiatric internment of dissidents, he clarified, "is not a misappropriation of psychiatry: it is its fundamental project."[33] The Soviet Union's continuity with the Western European past, previously conceived of in terms of its appropriation of bourgeois institutions and values, was now expressed in terms of its appropriation of disciplinary forms of power. Yet Foucault also recognized that important aspects of Soviet history did not fit into his disciplinary model: "terror, at its core, is not the height of discipline; it is its failure" and "the concentration camp was a middling option between the great terror and discipline."[34]

As the Gulag question grew in importance in France, Foucault found himself face to face with the inadequacy of his formulations and the need to clarify matters, which he did in an interview with Jacques Rancière in late 1977. Importantly, Foucault's motivation was political. Foucault feared that the rapprochement between the Gulag and what, in *Madness and Civilization*, he had called "the great confinement" might be used to make all persecutions appear alike, let the PCF off the hook, and allow the Left not to alter its discourse. The specificity of the Gulag had to be maintained, notably that "the Gulag is not a question to pose uniformly to any society whatsoever. It must be posed specifically to every socialist society insofar as none of them since 1917 has in fact managed to function without a more or less developed Gulag system."[35] Probably for these reasons, Foucault had references to the "carceral archipelago" removed from later editions of *Discipline and Punish*.[36]

Recognizing on some level that his model of disciplinary power was insufficient both in general and specifically to explain Soviet history, Foucault made a first effort to go beyond it in his 1976 Collège de France lectures. In his lecture of March 17, Foucault introduced the concept of "biopower," a new non-disciplinary technology of power that intervenes on the level of populations rather than individuals, via public health measures and the like, in order to regularize biological processes and thereby impact birth and death rates, the incidence of illnesses, etc., so as to improve the overall productivity and security of society. As political power increasingly turned toward biopower, making "its objective essentially to enable life," it was forced to turn to racism in order to justify killing, as "killing, the imperative to kill, is admissible in a system of biopower only if it does not aim at victory over political adversaries [which would be the case with traditional sovereign power], but at the elimination of the biological threat and the strengthening, directly linked to this elimination, of the species itself or of the race." In order to exercise its sovereign power to kill, a state must become racist, and also "in these conditions...the most murderous states are, at the same time, necessarily the most racist." After applying this analysis to Nazism – where it has some plausibility – Foucault then proceeds to apply it to Soviet history. Hedging his bets by recognizing that he was making "enormous claims" and that to prove his point would really require "another set of lectures," Foucault argues that socialism made no critique of biopower and was racist because, within the realm of biopower, racism is "the only way...to rationalize killing the adversary." Socialists "were racists to the extent that...they did not reevaluate – or accepted, if you like, as self-evident – these mechanisms of biopower that the development of society and the state since the eighteenth century had put in place."[37]

This analysis, which represents Foucault's most significant effort of the mid-1970s to analyze the power mechanisms at work in the Soviet Union, is inadequate on many levels. It presents no evidence of its claims and is entirely based on deduction following from Foucault's definition of biopower and his assumptions about its impact on the legitimization of state power. At no point does Foucault explain the obvious and most important issue, which is why certain states decide to kill in massive numbers and are able to do so. Nothing accounts for differences between state actors. They are all equally susceptible to becoming monstrous killing machines. That there might be mechanisms within some states that restrain them is not something that Foucault considers – at least not before 1978. States deploy disciplinary power and biopower, and they play active roles in the disciplining of knowledges, Foucault contends, but "it is not in calling upon sovereignty against discipline that one will be able to limit the very effects of disciplinary power."[38] This one-sided analysis of the state, which can do no good, may have been comforting to Foucault's fundamental anarchism, but it is too blunt an instrument to make sense of the twentieth century, as it provides no means by which to distinguish between different regimes – notably, dictatorial and democratic ones.[39] It left Foucault vulnerable to Glucksmann's argumentation because he lacked the conceptual tools to effectively critique his simplifications. In the end, it is this hole in Foucault's thought, as much as his political preferences and use of the mass media in his strategy of intellectual consecration, that explains his endorsement of Glucksmann and *The Master Thinkers*.

Notes

* This chapter is an expanded version of analysis originally published in M. S. Christofferson, *French Intellectuals against the Left: The Antitotalitarian Moment of the 1970s* (New York: Berghahn Books, 2004). The author thanks Berghahn Books for granting permission to republish.

1 Other factors contributed to their falling-out, such as disagreements on the Klaus Croissant case, the Israel–Palestine question, and the question of desire. See F. Dosse, *Gilles Deleuze et Félix Guattari. Biographie croisée* (Paris: La Découverte, 2007), 364–93.

2 Christofferson, *French Intellectuals against the Left*, ch. 5.

3 D. Eribon, *Michel Foucault (1926–1984)* (Paris: Flammarion, 1991), 336. Unless otherwise noted, translations are the author's own.

4 A. Glucksmann, *La cuisinière et le mangeur d'hommes. Essai sur l'État, le marxisme, et les camps de concentration* (Paris: Seuil, 1975), 173.

5 *Ibid.*, 109.

6 *Ibid.*, 112.

7 "De la violence: entretien avec André Glucksmann," *Actuel* 54 (May 1975): 17.

8 A. Glucksmann, *Les maîtres penseurs* (Paris: Grasset, 1977), 131, 290, 310.

9 *Ibid.*, 119, 128, 28, for the citations. This is a reference to the rule governing the Abbey of Thélème in François Rabelais's novel *Gargantua and Pantagruel*.

10 *Ibid.*, 117, 174, and 237 for the citations.

11 M. Foucault, "La grande Colère des faits," in his *Dits et écrits: 1954–1988*, vol. III, *1976–1979*, ed. D. Defert and F. Ewald with J. Lagrange (Paris: Gallimard, 1994), 277–81, and "Pouvoirs et stratèges," in *Dits et écrits*, vol. III, *1976–1979*, 421.

12 Glucksmann, *Les maîtres penseurs*, 309.

13 P. Dews, "The *nouvelle philosophie* and Foucault," *Economy and Society* 8, 2 (May 1979): 127–71, p. 142.

14 Dosse, *Gilles Deleuze et Félix Guattari*, 372.

15 E. Paras, *Foucault 2.0: Beyond Power and Knowledge* (New York: Other Press, 2006), 58.

16 According to Glucksmann, interviewed by James Miller: J. Miller, *The Passion of Michel Foucault* (New York: Anchor Books, 1993), 176.

17 Note though that Deleuze's public intervention in the debate on new philosophy discussed new philosophy in general, did not directly address Glucksmann's work, and said nothing of Foucault's endorsement of it. See G. Deleuze, "A propos des nouveaux philosophes et d'un problème plus général," *Minuit*, 24 (suppl.) (May 1977).

18 M. Foucault in "Les intellectuels et le pouvoir," in his *Dits et écrits: 1954–1988*, vol. II, *1970–1975*, ed. D. Defert and F. Ewald with J. Lagrange (Paris: Gallimard, 1994), 307–10; M. Foucault, "L'intellectuel sert à rassembler les idées mais son savoir est partiel par rapport au savoir ouvrier," in *Dits et écrits*, vol. II, *1970–1975*, 421–2.

19 M. Foucault in "Sur la justice populaire: débat avec les maos," in *Dits et écrits*, vol. II, *1970–1975*, 352–3. Foucault says, "And it [the bourgeoisie] thought it recognized in the non-proletarianized pleb, in the plebeians who refused the status of proletarian or those who were excluded from it, the spearhead of popular riots. It therefore put its energy into a certain number of methods to separate the proletarianized pleb from the non-proletarianized pleb."

20 Foucault, "Pouvoirs et stratèges," 421.

21 A. Glucksmann, "Le Marxisme rend sourd," *Le Nouvel Observateur* 486 (March 4, 1974): 80.

22 Glucksmann, *Les maîtres penseurs*, 227 and 223 for the citations. Pages 220 to 223 reprint Glucksmann's review of Clavel's *Dieu et Dieu* and his attack on the Union of the Left: "Les ballots du ballotage," *Le Monde*, April 9, 1976.

23 André Glucksmann interviewed by M. Gallo, *L'Express* 1358 (July 18, 1977): 62, 66–71.

24 In addition to the Gallo interview see his television appearances on *Questionnaire*, September 18, 1977, and *Apostrophes* on May 27, 1977, both consulted at the Institut national de l'audiovisuel. Glucksmann also discussed the significance of his book for the Left in *Libération*, May 27, 1977.

25 Eribon, *Michel Foucault*, 194.

26 M. Foucault, "Crimes et châtiments en U.R.S.S. et ailleurs,..." "Une mobilisation culturelle," and "La grille politique traditionnelle," in his *Dits et écrits*, vol. III, *1976–1979*, 79, 330–1, and 506–7; M. Clavel, "Vous direz trois rosaires," *Le Nouvel Observateur* 633 (December 27, 1977): 55; letter from Michel Foucault to Pierre Rosanvallon of December 17, 1977, provided to the author by Pierre Rosanvallon. Rosanvallon and Viveret were key intellectuals of the "Second Left." On Rosanvallon, Viveret, and their

co-authored book, see Christofferson, *Intellectuals against the Left*, 215–18. Also useful on Foucault and the Second Left in this period is chapter 2 in this volume, by Behrent.

27 M. Foucault, "Pouvoir et savoir," "Cours du 7 janvier 1976," and "Cours du 14 janvier 1976," in his *Dits et écrits*, vol. III, *1976–1979*, 400–1; 160–74, p. 167; 175–89, p. 181.

28 M. Foucault, "Non au sexe roi," "Pouvoirs et stratèges," and "Cours du 7 janvier 1976," in his *Dits et écrits*, vol. III, *1976–1979*, 266–7, 421–2, and 165 respectively.

29 M. Foucault, "Pouvoir et savoir," and "La Philosophie analytique de la politique," in Foucault, *Dits et écrits: 1954–1988*, vol. II, *1976–1988* (Paris: Gallimard, 2001), 400–2 and 555 respectively.

30 M. Foucault, "Conversation avec Michel Foucault," in his *Dits et écrits: 1954–1988*, vol. I, *1954–1975*, ed. D. Defert and F. Ewald with J. Lagrange (Paris: Gallimard, 2001), 1061.

31 M Foucault, "Par-delà le bien et le mal," in *ibid.*, 1102.

32 M. Foucault, *Surveiller et punir. Naissance de la prison* (Paris: Gallimard, 1975), 305. On the intention to refer to Solzhenitsyn, see "Questions à Michel Foucault sur la géographie," in his *Dits et écrits*, vol. III, *1976–1979*, 32.

33 M. Foucault, "Enfermement, psychiatrie, prison," in his *Dits et écrits*, vol. III, *1976–1979*, 334 and 335.

34 Foucault, "Crimes et châtiments en U.R.S.S. et ailleurs,..." 69.

35 M. Foucault, "Pouvoirs et stratèges," 418–20, p. 420.

36 This removal is noted by the editors of Foucault, "Questions à Michel Foucault sur la géographie," 32.

37 M. Foucault, *"Il faut défendre la société." Cours au Collège de France. 1975–1976* (Paris: Seuil/Gallimard, 1997), 227, 228, 230, 232–3, and 234 for the citations. In translating these passages I consulted and used some of the wording from, M. Foucault, *"Society Must be Defended": Lectures at the Collège de France, 1975–76*, trans. D. Macey (New York: Picador, 2003).

38 Foucault, *"Il faut défendre la société,"* 35.

39 A similar point is made from a different perspective by M. Walzer's "The Politics of Michel Foucault," in D. Couzens, ed., *Foucault: A Critical Reader* (Oxford and New York: Basil Blackwell, 1986), 51–86.

2

Liberalism without Humanism: Michel Foucault and the Free-Market Creed, 1976–1979

Michael C. Behrent

For some time now, Michel Foucault has been a familiar figure in American academic life. Graduate students in the humanities and social sciences are expected to master his dense tomes. His works have become staples of undergraduate courses, where their strange themes and cryptic formulations – the "death of the author," "power/knowledge," "bodies and pleasure" – can still elicit a frisson of intellectual subversion from the unsuspecting sophomore. Foucault's thought, moreover, has launched fleets of new disciplines and methodologies. His insights concerning the relationship between power and the human body have, for instance, been debated by a generation of feminist thinkers.[1] In queer theory, he has become so canonical a figure that a prominent scholar once remarked that "if Michel Foucault had never existed, queer politics would have had to invent him."[2] His shadow looms equally large over postcolonial studies: writing in 1995, Anne Stoler noted "that no single analytic framework has saturated the field of colonial studies so completely over the last decade as that of Foucault."[3] Guided by his signature concept of "discourse," historians negotiated the cultural and linguistic "turns" of the 1980s.[4] In Europe and the United States, an entire subdiscipline has arisen around a single term that Foucault coined in the late 1970s: "governmentality."[5]

Two scholarly journals have devoted themselves exclusively to his thought.[6]

Needless to say, not every word dedicated to Foucault has been hagiographic, or even sympathetic. Some feminists have detected overtones of misogyny in his work, while postcolonial theorists find his unreconstructed Eurocentrism troubling. No doubt he still has the capacity to enrage, as he did during the culture wars of the 1990s, when Camille Paglia could accuse Foucault of displaying the "same combination of maniacal abstraction with lust for personal power that led to the deranged orderliness of the concentration camps."[7] Yet, one suspects, those who can still summon up such vitriol are fighting the last academic war. Though it remains controversial, Foucault's voice has become, in the end, familiar: one, like that of Marx or Freud, which we recognize and accommodate, however radically it challenges our picture of the world.

Part of the reason for Foucault's familiarity is that we immediately grasp the political force of what he has to say. By unveiling the subtle but pervasive webs of powers that ensnare us, Foucault also suggested how we might disentangle ourselves from them. He offers, one may plausibly surmise, a politics of freedom – an initiation, as he once put it, to the "art of not being...governed."[8] We sense, intuitively, that his politics are emancipatory: though we know that he is no more a Marxist than a social democrat, we turn to him not so much to challenge as to enrich the palette of leftist social criticism. For Michel Foucault, as we imagine him, is most certainly a man of the Left. True, we have heard it rumored that he is a "young conservative";[9] we remember, perhaps, that a great philosopher once called Foucault "the last barrier that the bourgeoisie can still raise against Marx."[10] But most of us find such charges hard to take seriously. Could a thinker who divulged the repressive agenda lurking within well-meaning projects of social reform, who unmasked the exclusionary mechanisms of Enlightenment-inspired rationality, and who enjoined us to overcome our inner fascist be anything other than a Left-wing intellectual – albeit a brilliantly original one?

Yet the American academy's warm embrace of Foucault has come at a cost: that of a certain indifference to the historical contexts that shaped his work. The failure to consider the intimate relationship between Foucault's thought and the twists and turns of postwar French history has rendered his American audience occasionally tone-deaf to the character of his evolving political commitments. To be sure, the episodes in Foucault's career that most easily align with expectations concerning his political radicalism – one thinks, for instance, of his involvement in the "Prison Information Group" (Groupe d'information sur les prisons, or GIP) in the early 1970s – are relatively well known. Those junctures when Foucault defied these assumptions have received, however, far less attention. This is true of one critical moment in particular. In the late 1970s, the same Foucault whom academic radicals have lionized flirted with an outlook anchored on the political Right: the free-market creed known as neoliberalism. For his defenders, the notion that Foucault might have taken seriously a school of thought embraced by Ronald Reagan, Margaret Thatcher, and Alan Greenspan defies credibility. Yet Foucault's attraction to neoliberalism was real, and the logic of this interest understandable – provided that we grasp precisely what attracted him to it. This requires, however, a far more contextualized reading of his work than American Foucauldians are generally prepared to abide. Foucault's "neoliberal moment" must be situated in the broad shift of allegiances that transformed French intellectual politics in the 1970s – a topic that has recently attracted the attention of historians. The 1970s were a historical watershed in France, when many former radicals critiqued Marxism for its latent totalitarianism, nurtured a newfound admiration for liberalism, and professed their opposition to an electoral alliance uniting socialists and communists.[11] Yet while it is well known that Foucault publicly supported the so-called "new philosophers" in their assault on Marxism, the extent to which this shift impacted his own thinking has been underestimated. Foucault did not limit himself to placing his *imprimatur* on the new political outlook. He also innovated – a fact that becomes evident when one considers the lectures that he delivered between 1976 and 1979 at the Collège de France, in which Foucault presented his audiences with an idiosyncratic appraisal of economic liberalism.[12]

This crucial episode in Foucault's thought has been neglected in part because these lectures have only recently appeared in print. But an equally important factor is the unwillingness of many of his readers to hear what he is saying. This deafness takes several forms. Some of Foucault's critics assume that his thought is fundamentally incompatible with liberalism of any kind. This appreciation rests, in the first place, on the various ways in which his work purported to unveil the subtle forms of repression lurking within allegedly liberal societies. But the greatest obstacle on the Foucauldian path to liberalism is usually considered to be his philosophical antihumanism. And with good reason: antihumanism is in many respects the leitmotif of Foucault's entire intellectual enterprise, though it received its sharpest formulation in his famous prophecy of the "death of man" in 1966's *The Order of Things*. "Our task," Foucault once declared, "is to emancipate ourselves definitively from humanism."[13] Far from being Western culture's defining preoccupation, the problem of "man" (which he held to be synonymous with "humanism") was, Foucault contended, of recent vintage, dating only to the end of the eighteenth century (and thus had nothing in common, for instance, with Renaissance humanism). Far from being a moral affirmation of the inherent worth of human life and experience, humanism thus conceived is primarily epistemological: "man," he claimed, has become knowledge's ultimate horizon. Foucault's prediction of this paradigm's imminent demise was above all an assertion that the philosophical primacy given to the human subject – heretofore knowledge's transcendental condition – had exhausted itself. "Man is disappearing in philosophy," he explained in 1968, "not as an object of knowledge, but as the subject of liberty and of existence."[14] This concerted assault on humanism, "man," and the human subject would seem to preclude any affinity between Foucault and liberalism, a political philosophy that is usually taken to rest upon these very principles. On such grounds, the political philosopher Michael Walzer has argued, for instance, that Foucault's failure to offer an "an account... of the liberal state and the rule of law" contributes to "the catastrophic weakness of his political theory."[15] A different argument portrays Foucault as a liberal in denial: if he denounced Franco, defended the

Vietnamese boat people, and spoke out for the trade union
Solidarity when it was outlawed by the Polish government,
was it not because he subscribed, *sotto voce*, to some form
of crypto-liberalism? A number of historians maintain that,
in the 1970s, Foucault did indeed become a happy convert
to the philosophy of human rights. In this vein, Richard
Wolin remarks, "At the time of Foucault's death in 1984,
prominent observers noted the irony that the ex-structuralist
and 'death-of-man' prophet had played a pivotal role in
facilitating French acceptance of political liberalism."[16] Along
similar lines, Eric Paras paints the portrait of a Foucault who,
under the sway of "new philosophers," abandoned his philosophical antihumanism once it suddenly appeared insuffi-
ciently inoculated against totalitarianism. In a 1979 letter to
the Iranian prime minister, Paras points out, Foucault mentioned "human rights" no less than four times, and "rights"
an additional seven.[17]

Rather than parsing his words for some kind of secret
conversion, others have seen Foucault as engaged in a critical
dialogue with liberalism. Richard Rorty, for instance, suggested that Foucault's defense of autonomy was all the more
liberal in that it was antifoundationalist – that is, that it did
not claim to be derived from an underlying anthropological
or metaphysical truth.[18] According to John Rajchman, while
Foucault demonstrated that liberal freedoms belong to "a
disciplinary power figuration," the critical practices that he
brought to bear on power structures – including nominally
liberal ones – were motivated by emancipatory instincts.
"Our real freedom," Rajchman contends, "is found in dis-
solving or changing the polities that embody our nature."[19]
Foucault shows us, in short, that liberalism's main problem
is that it is not liberal enough.

In France, particularly since the publication of his lectures
from the late 1970s, one finds greater awareness of Foucault's
interest in economic liberalism. But even those who are familiar with these views often remain skeptical of the idea that
Foucault betrayed any sympathy for the forms of liberalism
he discussed. If they do refer to his views on neoliberalism,
they assume that he could only have intended to denounce it
as a new and sinister form of power. Thus Jeannette Colombel, for instance, asserts that in his 1979 lectures, Foucault

demonstrated that neoliberalism "constituted a dual society, in which the excluded, who are ever more numerous, remain passive."[20] Frédéric Lebaron asserts that Foucault "resisted the neoliberal turn, even if he did not truly perceive its depth and radicalism."[21] Judith Revel, a leading French Foucault scholar, makes a more nuanced case for the claim that Foucault's appraisal of neoliberalism was ultimately critical. While acknowledging the existence of "neoliberal readings" of Foucault, Revel, too, suggests that Foucault ultimately sought to conceptualize strategies for resisting the neoliberal order.[22] The view that Foucault staked out a largely negative position on neoliberalism is, of course, perfectly understandable, given that one of the most striking tendencies of his *oeuvre* is an effort to smoke out the hidden mechanisms of power afflicting modern societies. Yet these readings ultimately ask us to believe that Foucault meant something quite different from what he was saying – at least when he spoke of neoliberalism. We should begin, rather, by asking if Foucault's pronouncements make sense on their own terms.

For what these assessments of Foucault's relation to liberalism overlook is *what* he actually said about liberalism, and *how* his pronouncements on liberalism were a response to a very particular political moment. Liberalism, for Foucault, was hardly a marginal concern. It became – however briefly – the primary focus of two lecture series delivered at the Collège de France: one in 1978, entitled *Security, Population, and Territory*, and another the following year, on *The Birth of Biopolitics*. What both Foucault's critics and his defenders have failed to consider is a deep affinity between Foucault's thought and neoliberalism: a shared suspicion of the state. Foucault's antistatism was, in the first instance, theoretical. He famously complained that "in political thought and analysis, the king's head has still not been cut off."[23] What he meant was that political theorists too often understand power on the model of the state, viewing it as flowing top-down from a transcendent authority, rather than as a force disseminated across the social space through complex and open-ended relations, involving a wide range of actors and institutions. This position was a logical consequence of Foucault's antihumanism: the main fallacy of state-based models of politics is that they anthropomorphize power by viewing it as the conscious expression of a will. The theoretical anti-statism implicit in Foucault's thought required, however, a specific configuration of circumstances to be actualized. In the 1970s, however, Foucault's theoretical antistatism became increasingly normative: his claim that we should abandon the state as our model for understanding power evolved, in other words, into an argument that the state should cease to be the primary focus of engaging in politics. The context in which this shift occurred is both significant and underappreciated. The economic crisis that struck France in 1973, accompanied by the implosion of the statist assumptions that had driven the country's remarkable postwar growth, suddenly made economic liberalism far more relevant to public discourse than it had been for decades. Spurred by these events, Foucault seems to have recognized the affinity between his theoretical objection to state-based conceptions of power and the economic liberalism that was the subject of contemporary debates. The onset of prolonged economic malaise in the early 1970s, I argue, proves to be as critical a factor in the intellectual transformations of the 1970s as antitotalitarianism or the so-called "death of Marx."

Thus Foucault did indeed have a liberal moment – but it was inspired not by the *political* liberalism of Benjamin Constant, Alexis de Tocqueville, or François Guizot, whom other intellectuals were busily dusting off at the time, but by *economic* liberals like Adam Smith, Wilhelm Röpke, and the Chicago School. In his 1978 and 1979 lectures, the anti-statism latent in Foucault's theory of power was nurtured by the resurgence of neoliberal ideas that the 1973 economic crisis precipitated. In this climate, Foucault found economic liberalism to be intellectually appealing for two crucial reasons. First, at a juncture when he, like a number of his contemporaries, was attempting to free French intellectual life from the headlock of revolutionary leftism (or *gauchisme*), economic liberalism proved to be a potent theoretical weapon for bludgeoning the Left's authoritarian proclivities. Second, Foucault could endorse economic liberalism because, unlike its political counterpart, it did not require him to embrace philosophical humanism – the outlook that Foucault had, from the outset of his career, contested with all the energy that his intellectual skills could muster. The theoretical condition of possibility of Foucault's neoliberal moment was his insight that economic liberalism is, essentially, a liberalism without humanism. The limitation of state power that defines the practice of economic liberalism does not occur, Foucault maintained, when "subjects" are recognized as having "rights." Of such hypotheses it has no need. Rather, economic liberalism justifies itself on the basis of its greater efficiency: it is a practice that arises when power realizes that it has an interest *as* power in *limiting* power. Far from being grounds for denouncing it, this is precisely why Foucault found economic liberalism so appealing: it offered a compelling terrain upon which his practical aspiration for freedom might merge with his theoretical conviction that power is constitutive of all human relationships. Once this is grasped, moreover, it becomes possible to preempt the tendency to see Foucault's fascination with liberalism as anticipating or accompanying his burgeoning interest in subjectivity (to which the final volumes of *The History of Sexuality* bear witness), a view which rests on the premise that liberal politics and the human subject necessarily imply one another.[24] In these ways, Foucault's liberal moment confounds the assumption, shared by both his defenders and his detractors, that liberalism and humanism are philosophically inseparable. Paradoxical though it may sound, one merit of examining how Foucault engaged with the vagaries of contemporary politics is that it throws into relief how unwaveringly committed he remained to his core philosophical beliefs. Thus his exploration of economic liberalism, a matter on which he had previously said next to nothing,[25] ended up revealing just how deep his antihumanism ran. That precisely these commitments led him to succumb to economic liberalism's charms should give pause to his friends and foes alike.

The 1970s watershed: the discreet charm of economic liberalism

Foucault's late 1970s flirtation with economic liberalism was one sign among many of the broad realignment in French intellectual politics under way in that decade. Like many of his contemporaries, Foucault was finding it increasingly difficult to hide his exasperation with the toll that Marxism had taken on intellectual and political life. In 1978 he denounced the tendency of intellectuals of the post-1968 era toward "hyper-Marxism" – that is, "the pulverization of Marxism into little bodies of doctrine" with less and less to say about vital political issues.[26] The writer Claude Mauriac recalls that, during a demonstration in 1975, the philosopher was invited to say a few impromptu words about the founder of modern socialism. Foucault impatiently replied, "Don't talk to me about Marx any more. I never want to hear of that gentleman again. Go and talk to the professionals. The ones who are paid to do that. The ones who are his civil servants. For my part, I'm completely through with Marx."[27] Meanwhile, Foucault was effusive in his praise of the anti-Marxist "new philosophers," the most vocal spokespersons of the emerging political sensibility.[28]

Yet Foucault's liberal turn was not only directed against Marxism. It also occurred in the midst of one of the decisive turning points of contemporary French history: the economic crisis of the early 1970s. Though the crisis was sparked by OPEC's decision to triple (and later quadruple) oil prices in October 1973, historians now agree that industrialized nations had been teetering on the edge of a precipice at least since August 1971, when Richard Nixon abruptly ended the gold convertibility of the dollar, felling one of the main pillars of the international financial system established at Bretton Woods in 1944. The result was more than a temporary downturn: as Jeffrey A. Frieden puts it, nothing less than the "postwar era ended in the early 1970s."[29] This certainly was the case in France. For much of the period between 1944 and the early 1970s, unprecedented growth, high levels of employment, and a dramatic rise in living standards had been propelled by a perfect storm of demographic expansion, American reconstruction aid, European integration, and state planning, among other factors.[30] By late 1973, however, the *trente glorieuses* (or "thirty glorious years") – as the economist Jean Fourastié dubbed them in an eponymous obituary for this age – were grinding to a halt.[31] Defaulting to the Keynesian axioms that had served Western economies so well since the war, the French government sought in 1974 to curtail the rising tide of inflation, but managed only to stall growth.

Switching gears, the government attempted, the following year, to stimulate the economy, but still found itself faced with nearly a million unemployed.[32] As Fourastié observed in late 1973, the "easy times" of the postwar years had come and gone.[33]

Even as stagflation and mass unemployment disrupted French society – strikes prompted by layoffs proliferated between 1974 and 1975 – they also confounded the economic orthodoxies that had prevailed during the postwar period, notably the "stop-and-go" policies (that is, using fiscal policy to rein in inflation and stimulate growth during a recession) associated with Keynesian theory. In 1976, Jacques Rueff, perhaps France's most distinguished liberal economist, hailed in *Le Monde* "The End of the Keynesian Era." According to Rueff, it was the "Cambridge magician" himself who was ultimately responsible for the contemporary turmoil: by persuading postwar governments that, through investment, they could end unemployment and expand their economies, Keynes's doctrine "opened wide the floodgates of inflation and unemployment" – scourges, he presaged, that are "destroying before our eyes what remains of Western civilization."[34]

In this crisis atmosphere, liberal economists, who had been sidelined by Keynesians in many industrial countries for much of the postwar period, were given a second look. Nor would they have long to wait for electoral victory: Margaret Thatcher would triumph in Britain's 1979 general election, while in the United States Ronald Reagan was gearing up the campaign that would win him the presidency. In France, free-market liberals got an even earlier crack at resolving the crisis. Seeking a way out of the country's economic impasse, President Valéry Giscard d'Estaing (himself a former finance minister of liberal proclivities) turned to Raymond Barre, a liberal economist and translator of Friedrich Hayek, the Austrian guru of neoliberalism,[35] appointing him prime minister in August 1976. After his initial anti-inflation plan achieved only moderate results, Barre seized on the right's unexpected victory in the 1978 parliamentary elections to pursue a more ambitious agenda – one specifically inspired by liberal principles. The centerpiece of Barre's plan was the elimination of long-standing price caps on a wide range of goods and services, many of which had existed since 1945. Of greatest symbolic importance was the deregulation of the price of bread, notably the hallowed baguette.[36] These measures notwithstanding, Barre's economic liberalism was hardly extreme. Appraising his policies, the economist André Fourçans observed in 1979 that Barre's policies did not represent a "return to the 'savage capitalism' of the nineteenth century," but rather an effort "to run counter to the French state's tradition of *dirigisme* and niggling interventionism in order to give an important place back to market mechanisms."[37] Indeed, purists have derided Barre's liberalism as half-baked, as he also presided over significant increases in social spending to placate those constituencies that the crisis had hit hardest.[38] His experiments were, moreover, short-lived: just as free-marketeers were sailing to power in Britain and the United States, the French elected, in 1981, a socialist president promising a "rupture with capitalism." Even so, it is remarkable that, in a country well known for its statist traditions, a French prime minister proved something of a trailblazer in the broad reorientation of economic policy under way in industrialized nations at the time. By ushering in what has been described as "pragmatic" or "proto-" neoliberalism,[39] Barre's tenure, it has been argued, spelled in many ways "the end of the 'French model'."[40] This was not lost on contemporaries: in 1979, the prime minister's ideas reportedly found an admiring audience in Thatcher's new government.[41]

However one judges his success, Barre in any case contributed to the rehabilitation of economic liberalism as a plausible theoretical framework. Writing for *Le Monde* in October 1978, Pierre Drouin observed that "the notion of the market has recovered a luster that it has not known for a long time."[42] This liberal renaissance drew on France's often unacknowledged but nonetheless robust tradition of economic liberalism, which the French affinity for state intervention has often occluded.[43] Monica Prasad argues that, while far from dominant, neoliberalism emerged as "an important minority position in 1970s France."[44] It had, for instance, infiltrated the inner circles of France's academic elite. Students at the École nationale d'administration (ENA), the premier institution for top civil servants, were taught by Jean-Jacques Rosa, a staunch neoliberal economist who was convinced that "bulimic states" were to blame for the illnesses afflicting Western economies. His ideas struck a chord, as one authority has argued: "The high bureaucrats rising from the ENA or from the École polytechnique [the top engineering school] believe that there is a limit to the state's intervention and to the tax burden. The state can't do everything, it has already done too much, it should stop."[45] Nearby, at the prestigious Institut d'études politiques, Jacques Rueff, the dean of French economic liberalism, taught alongside a group known as the "new economists" (including Jean Fourastié, Jean-Marie Benoist, Lionel Stoléru, Jean-Pierre Fourcade, and André Fourçans), who shared his commitment to free markets.[46] A number of essays touting liberal solutions to the economic turmoil appeared in the mid- to late 1970s, particularly to dissuade voters from opting for the Socialist–Communist alliance in the 1978 elections.[47] At the same time, publishers hurriedly translated the works of Milton Friedman and Hayek into French,[48] while in 1980 Presses Universitaires de France launched a series entitled *Libre échange* (Free Trade), which introduced Thomas Sowell, Irving Kristol, and Robert Nozick to the French public. The same year, Hayek himself regaled a French audience with his wisdom in an address at the National Assembly.[49] Thus when Foucault noted that "American neoliberalism" had, by 1979, become a tad clichéd ("une tarte à la crème"), he was only slightly exaggerating.[50]

A particularly prominent spokesman for a liberal solution to the crisis was a young economist named Henri Lepage, who seized the public's attention in 1978 with an essay entitled *Demain le capitalisme* (Tomorrow, Capitalism). The book was a pithy primer to recent American economic theory, including the work of University of Chicago economists Gary Becker and Milton Friedman, "public-choice" economists such as James M. Buchanan, "human-capital" theorists, and libertarians – many of the same economists whom Foucault would consider in his lectures the following year. But the essay was also a vigorous polemic targeting the entrenched prejudice against economic thought, particularly in its liberal form, that pervaded French intellectual culture.[51] An aversion to economics, he suggested, was ultimately responsible for the absurdities that, on the Left, passed for a political agenda.

"The true danger" that France faces, Lepage warned, "comes less from the discourse and the palinodes of François Mitterrand and [Communist Party leader] Georges Marchais, than from this deep-seated intellectual intoxication which, little by little, habituates an entire sector of the intelligentsia and of French opinion to think, often without realizing it, in 'Marxian' terms."[52] At a time when disillusionment with Marxism was spawning interest in political liberalism, Lepage, sensing the moment was ripe, sought to persuade his readers that human rights logically implied free markets:

> those who defend liberalism on a political level [must become] conscious of the tight bonds that unite liberal philosophy to the scientific foundations of *capitalist* society. Those who adhere to a liberal philosophy must cease to have a guilty conscience because of this connection between liberalism and capitalism and devote sufficient effort to rediscovering the theoretical and scientific arguments as to why this guilty conscience has no reason to exist.[53]

In other words, no Tocqueville without Milton Friedman. But Lepage took his argument a step further: not only are economic and political liberalism inseparable, but the former guarantees freedom far more securely than the latter. Why? Because markets wean us from the belief that freedom's primary locus lies in politics. The prospect that the state – or at least, the mindset that privileges the state – could wither away is, Lepage contended, perhaps the most exhilarating implication of the new American economics, which demonstrates that "the State is not, as one has too often the tendency to see it, a divine construction, endowed with the gift of ubiquity and infallibility."[54]

Antistatist sentiment of this kind was not, however, confined to the Right. Lepage's arguments found an unlikely echo from a current that one would not typically suspect of sympathizing with economic liberalism: the so-called "Second Left." An important minority current in French socialism, closely associated with the Unified Socialist Party (Parti socialiste unifié, or PSU), a small party led by Michel Rocard, and the French Democratic Confederation of Labor (Confederation française démocratique du travail; CFDT), a major trade union, the Second Left (as it has become known) was also profoundly antistatist – though its immediate target was mainstream socialism's (i.e. the "First Left's") fixation on the state, rather than interventionism as such. Thus, in a 1975 manifesto, Edmond Maire, the CFDT's leader, and the journalist Jacques Julliard outlined their vision of a society that would "decompose and redistribute" the functions of the capitalist state, transforming its "shackles" into a "voluntary institution."[55] Critical to the Second Left's outlook was its concept of *autogestion* ("self-management"), which articulated its conviction that society could govern itself without the mediation of oppressive institutions, of which the modern state was the most glaring instance. Though much of the PSU fused with François Mitterrand's newly reconstructed Socialist Party in 1974, the Second Left's antistatist alternative to traditional socialism continued to resonate with the post-1968 mood. By the mid-1970s it had blossomed into a major intellectual force, with its own journal, *Faire*, and a principal theorist, Pierre Rosanvallon. The Second Left's ascendancy was also a reflection of the political context: at a time when Mitterrand's socialists seemed constantly on the verge of electoral victory (including near misses in 1974 and 1978), the Second Left's partisans strove to free the party from what they called "social statism," lest a victory of progressive forces result in a reassertion of knee-jerk *dirigisme*.

Though firmly anchored in the Left's vision of social progress, the Second Left's outlook overlapped in significant (if limited) ways with that of the newly strident economic liberals, insofar as both identified an overdependence on the state as one of French society's primary weaknesses. At times, the Second Left and economic liberals appeared to be cautiously courting one another. Thus, in 1976, Rosanvallon wrote, "The *autogestionnaire* proposition…resonates with the liberal project of limiting the state's power and of a power that belongs to civil society."[56] Two years later, Lepage toyed with recruiting the very audiences that Rosanvallon was addressing when he mused, "Liberals will have succeeded when they have convinced some of those who, on the Left, reject collectivism as much as contemporary capitalism that the solution to the ills they denounce depends precisely on Capitalism."[57] In the inaugural issue of *Commentaire* (a journal destined to become a leading voice of the liberal resurgence), Jean Baechler confessed, upon completing a thorough analysis of Rosanvallon's ideas, "I am unable to perceive the slightest difference between a pure liberal system and a pure self-managed [*autogéré*] system; they clearly share the same project, the presentation and coloration of which vary in relation to the historical references [offered]."[58] In the end, however, critiquing the state did not prove a broad enough basis for achieving a lasting rapprochement between these tendencies. Rosanvallon went out of his way to stress that *autogestion*'s deep ties were to political, not economic, liberalism;[59] Lepage authored a detailed refutation of *autogestionnaire* economics.[60] Even so, at a time when the state-centered policies of the Keynesian era were under attack, an at least partial convergence between the liberal Right and the *autogestionnaire* Left was occurring under the banner of antistatism.

Foucault's interest in neoliberalism appears to owe much to his attraction to the Second Left. In 1977, Rosanvallon sent Foucault a copy of *Pour une nouvelle Culture politique* (For a New Political Culture), an essay in which he and Patrick Viveret explored *autogestionnaire* alternatives to both contemporary capitalism and statist socialism. Foucault replied with an enthusiastic letter, praising the authors for their "remarkable perception" of the present and for proposing an analysis that was trenchant without being "immobilizing."[61] The same year, Rosanvallon (who later participated in Foucault's research seminars at the Collège de France) organized a conference on "The Left, Experimentation, and Social Change," which Foucault attended, along with some 200 other participants, including intellectuals like Ivan Illich and Alain Touraine, and sympathetic socialists such as Jacques Delors and Michel Rocard. After attending a workshop on neighborhood medical services, Foucault, in an interview, approved the participants' grassroots politics, as well as the noticeable absence of Marxist cant, which he welcomed as evidence of the "disappearance of terrorism, of theoretical monopolies, and of the monarchy of accepted thinking."[62] The critique of statism was, moreover, clearly an integral part of the participants' vision of social change. In an article about the conference written for *Le Nouvel Observateur*,

Rosanvallon announced that the time had come "to de-stateify [*désetatiser*] society" and to abandon mainstream socialism's "centralist conception of social transformation."[63] Foucault's interest in economic liberalism, it would seem, was spurred more by his interest in Left-wing alternatives to "social statism" than by overt sympathy for Thatcher, Reagan, or Barre. Yet, over time, the critique of French socialism meant that some of the Second Left's adherents could, if not accept, at least entertain liberal economic arguments to a degree that would have been unthinkable in other sectors of the Left. Thus Rosanvallon, disputing the claim that contemporary economic liberals were merely spouting "traditional bour-geois ideology," observed in 1981, "These works have their coherence. In a context in which economic and social thought of Marxist origin has run out of steam, they do not lack a force of conviction. They have a real capacity of intellectual seduction."[64]

Thus in the 1970s, while some intellectual paradigms were on their way out, others were on their way in. At the very moment when intellectuals were airing their grievances with Marxism, the economic crisis, by exposing the limitations of postwar economic orthodoxies, handed free-market liberals their biggest soapbox in decades. In the debates accompany-ing these shifts, a recurring motif was the critique of French statism – a concern shared by free-market liberals and Second Left socialists, despite otherwise profound disagreements. Yet while context goes a long way in explaining why Fou-cault lectured on economic liberalism in 1978 and 1979, the sufficient cause lies in his own evolving philosophical posi-tion. For the various forms of antistatism emerging in the 1970s resonated in provocative ways with a central plank of his theoretical program: the effort to conceptualize power without reference to the state.

1976–1978: revising the "disciplinary hypothesis"

By 1976, Foucault was increasingly concerned that the views he had defended in *Discipline and Punish* were in need of revision. In his genealogy of the modern prison, Foucault cautioned that the seemingly humanitarian attitudes motivating nineteenth-century penal reform represented, in reality, an insidious new form of power that he called "discipline," which individualizes subjects the better to survey their bodies, normalize their behavior, and regulate their movement. In disciplinary society, the prison is, if not the dominant institution, then certainly the exemplary one, both because other institutions (such as schools, the military, and hospitals) emulate its procedures, and because, by systematically reproducing the very criminals that it is charged with reforming, it continually reinforces the disciplinary regime's *raison d'être.* Yet shortly after the book's publication in 1975, Foucault began to question his core assumption that discipline is political modernity's signal trait. A close reading of his Collège de France lecture courses of the late 1970s leaves little doubt that he believed his views on discipline were in need of significant qualification. Ultimately, this enterprise would dovetail with his exploration of economic liberalism.

Foucault's first step in revising the "disciplinary hypothesis" (to use Eric Paras's apt phrase) was taken in the 1976 course, in which Foucault divested discipline of its status as power's most contemporary form. In *Discipline and Punish* Foucault had argued that, with the modern carceral system, disciplinary power reaches a high-water mark. He describes, for instance, the Mettray prison, which opened in 1840, as inaugurating "an art of punishing that is still more or less our own."[65] In the book's famous concluding footnote, Foucault proposed that his study might "serve as a historical background to various studies of the power of normalization and the formation of knowledge in modern society," thus confirming his belief that the prison system and contemporary power were closely intertwined.[66] Yet by early 1976, Foucault had begun to question his earlier position. On March 17, he argued that during the eighteenth century, a new form of power appeared, which, without completely replacing discipline, nonetheless operated on considerably different principles. He proposed to name it "biopolitics" or "biopower." In this lecture, which is in many respects a rough draft of the final chapter of *The History of Sexuality: An Introduction,*[67] Foucault distinguishes biopower from two earlier forms: sovereignty and discipline. According to early modern theories of sovereignty, power is never more itself than when it takes the life of its subjects. Yet by the nineteenth century, power defines itself less by ending life than by advancing it – through the production of wealth, the promotion of public health, and, in general, the maximization of a population's life forces. The latter – which is biopower – seeks, as Foucault famously puts it, to "make live and let die," where the earlier form strove to "let live and make die." Yet this transition from sovereignty to biopower involves, Foucault claims, an intermediary step: discipline. Discipline, Foucault reminds his audience, targets individual bodies, organizing them into "a field of visibility" through technologies of surveillance and inspection, while optimizing their utility through practices of exercise and "training" (*dressage*).[68] Yet barely a year after the publication of the book in which he presented these ideas, Foucault now limited discipline's reign to the seventeenth and eighteenth centuries, rather than making it coterminous with modernity itself. For with the development of biopower in the eighteenth century, Foucault explains, "something new" was happening: the emergence of a "nondisciplinary" technology of power.[69] Where discipline governs "the multiplicity of men" insofar as it can be "resolved into individual bodies," biopower administers the "mass as a whole," aggregated into a "population."[70] Moreover, unlike discipline, biopower's concern is not with individual conduct, but with general "states of equilibrium [and] of regularity" in the population as a whole.[71] Foucault does, it is true, acknowledge that discipline and biopower frequently overlap: the latter does not so much replace the former as "envelop" and "integrate" it, transforming discipline by "implanting itself... within it."[72] Because they operate on different levels – one being aimed at individuals, the other at populations – they can, moreover, "articulate themselves on one another" – witness the power mechanisms at work in urban management and sexuality.[73] Yet even as he stressed their compatibility, Foucault, by introducing biopower, stepped back from the expansive claims that he had previously made for discipline, opening himself up to an alternative understanding of contemporary politics.

Yet Foucault's revision of the disciplinary hypothesis did not stop here. In his 1978 lecture series (he did not teach in 1977), Foucault began to emphasize the relationship between biopower and liberalism – an insight that undermined his claim that discipline was merely "enveloped" by biopower. At the very moment when free-market ideas were influencing economic debates – and as Barre was competing against socialists and communists for control of the National Assembly – Foucault came to the conclusion that many of biopower's most exemplary traits were exhibited by economic liberalism. In 1978, however, he opted to consider the Physiocrats, a school of proto-liberal French economists from the eighteenth century, rather than economic liberalism's more contemporary avatars. What the Physiocrats demonstrate, Foucault maintained, is that whereas power directed at individuals (i.e. discipline) can expand almost ad infinitum, power aimed at populations (i.e. biopower) must learn to limit itself. Far from enveloping discipline, Physiocratic biopolitics stands in striking contrast to it: where discipline "regulates everything," Physiocracy, as much as possible, "laisse faire" – it lets things be.[74] "Letting things be" – or "laissez-faire," as the Physiocrats themselves called it, coining a phrase that would become the mantra of economic liberals everywhere – is another way of saying "freedom": for the Physiocratic art of governing is inconceivable in a society that lacks it, at least insofar as freedom is understood as noninterference. Freedom was, for instance, indispensable to the Physiocrats' approach to ending grain shortages. Cautioning against the disciplinary instinct that would impose price caps and force peasants to bring their grain to market, they proposed to abolish price controls across the board: tempted by the profits that they hoped to make from an ensuing spike in prices, hoarders and foreign exporters would flood the market with grain – which, in turn, would lower prices and feed the hungry. What Physiocracy's approach to managing grain shortages revealed, in short, was the basic insight of liberalism: one governs best by governing least. In his 1978 lectures, Foucault thus distanced himself even further from the disciplinary hypothesis: first, in claiming that economic liberalism is a paradigmatic form of biopower, he increasingly contrasted biopower to discipline, while highlighting the latter's archaic character; second, he suggested that, contrary to the thesis of *Discipline and Punish*, modern forms of power must give ample room to freedom. In Foucault's reasoning, these two claims are in fact connected: it is precisely because economic liberalism is not primarily concerned with individuals that, paradoxically, it offers individual freedom greater scope.

But could Foucault really have intended that his audience take the Physiocrats at their word? Is "freedom" not the product of an internalization of power's imperatives, and thus a form of *assujettissement* – that is, a process whereby one becomes a *subject* (an "I") only through being *subjected* to an external force? In *Discipline and Punish* Foucault certainly suggested as much. He presented the panopticon as the archetype of disciplinary power precisely because it minimizes recourse to physical constraint, in ways fully compatible with liberal conceptions of freedom. Freedom under discipline, he had suggested, is not the real thing: because it "never intervenes," because it is "exercised spontaneously and without noise," the panopticon creates an illusion of liberty, even as it wields power more effectively than any form preceding it.[75] Panoptic power does this by "creating" subjectivity: the individual placed within its "field of visibility, and who knows it, assumes responsibility for the constraints of power;...he becomes the principle of his own subjection [*assujettissement*]."[76] These are, of course, the very claims that are invoked to argue that Foucault could not be a liberal in any conventional sense. Yet in his 1978 course, Foucault makes a startling confession. He had once argued, he admitted,

> that one could not understand the establishment of liberal ideologies and politics in the eighteenth century without keeping in mind that this same eighteenth century, which had demanded these liberties so forcefully, had nonetheless weighed them down with a disciplinary technique which, taking children, soldiers, workers where they were, limited liberty considerably and in a sense gave guarantees to the very exercise of this liberty.[77]

But now, he adds, "Well, I believe that I was wrong." This was no minor correction: Foucault had, in effect, disowned a central argument of *Discipline and Punish*. That work, he recognized, had failed to take full measure of liberty's place in the modern economy of power. Liberty is not just a sleight of hand allowing power to operate with greater stealth, nor is it a form of false consciousness arising from *assujettisse-ment*. What biopower in the form of economic liberalism demonstrates is that liberty is power's necessary correlate – its very condition of possibility.

Foucault's reasons for taking liberty seriously are thus hardly designed to satisfy most liberals – and are, by the same token, remarkably consistent with his own philosophical commitments. Liberty matters politically, Foucault contends, once power ceases to target individuals (i.e. by creating "subjects"), and begins instead to manage populations. While Eric Paras is right to argue that Foucault abandoned his disciplinary hypothesis, it is misleading to suggest, as he does, that Foucault did so by rehabilitating the individual. It was Foucault's turn to biopolitics, particularly once he grasped its relation to economic liberalism, which led him to revise the disciplinary hypothesis, not his interest in ancient arts of living. Recognizing this is critical for resolving the thorny question of Foucault's relationship with liberalism. Foucault's critics – and many of his apologists – assume that his position on liberalism could only evolve in tandem with his views on individuality. Whatever such an assumption's inherent merits, Foucault simply did not agree: his increasingly positive appraisal of liberalism in no way entailed a rehabilitation of the "individual," the "subject," or – a fortiori – the "human." Foucault was fascinated by economic liberalism because, in his mind, it made far fewer anthropological claims than political liberalism, which he was happy to snub for the rest of his life. This is not to say Foucault was indifferent to the philosophical question of individuality; his more perceptive readers make it abundantly clear that he was not.[78] But in 1978, Foucault arrived at the position that when power targets populations, it can be significantly more accommodating of individual freedom than when, as with discipline, it places the individual squarely within its cross hairs. Consequently, far from representing power's ultimate tendency in modern society, the panopticon, Foucault now argued, is "the oldest dream of the oldest sovereign."[79] The disciplinary ideal of a completely visible social space that created subjects complicit in their own subjection belonged to the past – replaced by a form of power that aspires not to exhaustive knowledge of each individual, but to an understanding of the broad regularities governing a population.

The 1979 course: antihumanist liberalism and the critique of socialism

Despite being entitled *The Birth of Biopolitics*, Foucault's 1979 course was entirely devoted to liberal economic thought. Striking an apologetic tone, Foucault, in his opening lecture, confessed, "I had thought I would be capable of giving you this year a course on biopolitics." But in keeping with his arguments from the previous year, he nevertheless intended to show that it is only by understanding the "governmental regime called liberalism that one will be able...to grasp what biopolitics is."[80] In the 1979 course, Foucault never satisfactorily explained how he understood liberalism to be related to biopolitics. In his course summary, he claimed that he had intended to consider liberalism merely as an introduction to the broader question of biopolitics, since liberalism is the "framework" to which biopolitics presented its "challenge."[81] This would suggest that liberalism was opposed to biopolitics, and indeed to the task of governing as such. Yet Foucault nonetheless insisted on defining liberalism – as he had in his 1978 lectures – as a "technology of government," albeit one founded on the presumption of its own superfluity.[82] No doubt as a result of this ambiguity, the term "biopolitics" is largely absent from a course that is explicitly dedicated to it. Foucault's reasons for eliding it were, it would seem, twofold. First, he appears to have concluded that it is in economic liberalism, rather than in what he had previously called biopower, that the modern practice of power finds its most coherent expression. Second, at a time of economic crisis, shifting political allegiances, the emergence of a Left critique of statist socialism, and a broader rehabilitation of free-market economics, economic liberalism suddenly appeared extremely topical. "The problem of liberalism," Foucault explained in the year's first lecture, "finds itself actually posed in our immediate and concrete present."[83] But Foucault's lectures were more than glorified journalism.

They constituted a significant intervention in contemporary intellectual politics, in which Foucault sought, on the one hand, to challenge the philosophical basis upon which the liberal resurgence was occurring, and, on the other, to use economic liberalism as a vantage point from which to attack French socialism's unreconstructed statism.

Foucault's efforts to distance himself from the liberal renewal then under way are evident in a startling claim made in his January 17, 1979 lecture. Liberalism is historically significant, he asserts, because it dispenses with the notion that political authority must be founded in law. In the late 1970s this assertion presumably struck many as absurd: liberalism's appeal lay precisely in its efforts to subordinate political authority to the rule of law and the respect of human rights. In refuting law's centrality to liberalism, Foucault was challenging the project of François Furet and his collaborators (including Claude Lefort, Cornelius Castoriadis, Pierre Manent, Marcel Gauchet, and Pierre Rosanvallon[84]), who at the time were fashioning a non-Marxist account of the French Revolution, while using the categories of liberalism and democracy to build a novel theory of political modernity. According to Foucault, those who associate liberalism with law and rights fail to see that liberalism has developed along two distinct paths. The first, rooted in natural law, does indeed deduce the liberal state from the axiomatic assertion of inalienable individual rights. This path ultimately leads to the French Revolution. This form of liberalism rests, he notes, on the problematic assumption that where there is a law, there is a will: law is understood as the "expression of a will," particularly of a "collective will" which decrees (among other things) which rights individuals refuse to cede to the state. Law, in this tradition, is thus inextricably bound up with subjectivity (insofar as law is taken as expressing a will). The second path to liberalism is, however, grounded in utilitarianism: rather than deducing an ideal state from metaphysical principles, it takes the existence of government as a given, and, on the basis of purely inductive considerations, concludes that liberalism – that is, the self-limitation of power – simply makes the most administrative sense. This type of liberalism has no truck with the anthropological principles upon which the former is dependent – and which Foucault had always found suspect. From the utilitarian perspective, law is simply a process of "deal-making" (*transaction*), whereby individuals negotiate what powers belong to the state, and what freedoms they reserve for themselves. Where revolutionary liberalism makes law the foundation of politics, utilitarian liberalism sees politics as the origin of law. Having demonstrated how the tradition of political liberalism that emphasizes human rights and the legal basis of the state remained wedded to a problematic set of anthropological assumptions, Foucault could downplay the French Revolution's importance, dismissing its conception of politics as "retroactive"[85] – a charge, presumably, that he would have just as happily leveled against Furet and his cohort.[86]

In addition to dispensing with unnecessary anthropological hypotheses, utilitarian liberalism – alongside economic liberalism, which he considered to be closely related – impressed Foucault for another reason: it managed to conceptualize a liberal order by relying on no other category than power itself. For liberalism to work, Foucault suggested, there is no need to hypothesize something outside or beyond power, such as law, rights, or even liberty. Rather than a metaphysical entity or a human attribute, liberty, for the utilitarian, is simply a side-effect of power – as Foucault put it, "the independence of the governed in relation to the governing."[87] Similarly, for economic liberals, the paradoxical imperative that power must limit itself is essentially a political maxim aimed at optimizing administrative efficiency, not a morally motivated recognition of an inalienable right. Liberalism, Foucault explained, "is shot through with the principle: '*On gouverne toujours trop*'" – one always governs too much.[88] As we have seen, such a characterization of liberalism was, in the late 1970s, very much in the air: Foucault's definition echoes, in striking terms, Barre's pronouncement that "the State must do on its own as little as possible."[89] But this assessment was also consonant with Foucault's philosophical ambition to emancipate the conceptualization of power from juridical categories – or, as he liked to put it, to cut off the king's head (by abandoning the idea that power must derive from a sovereign, legitimate source). Because utilitarian and economic liberalism attach no special importance to the question of power's origin (unlike the revolutionary and natural-rights tradition), they effectively dispense with the need for juridical foundations.[90] Consequently, from Foucault's perspective, they manage to chop off the king's head very ably – more so, paradoxically, than the revolutionaries themselves. Contemporary economic liberalism thus epitomized power as Foucault had come to understand it. Just as for Marx the struggle between the bourgeoisie and the proletariat is both class conflict's latest form and the moment at which class conflict is unveiled as history's driving force, so liberalism is, for Foucault, both one form of power among others, and the form that demonstrates most effectively how little power has to do with law.

Economic and utilitarian liberalism thus suggested ways that one might be a liberal without subscribing to philosophical humanism or to a juridical theory of power. But if this explains how Foucault *could* be a liberal, what made him *want* to be one – or, in any event, to endorse it in a particular strategic context? The reason lies in Foucault's aversion to the stubborn archaism of the French Left, particularly as it was embodied by Mitterrand's Socialist Party. As Michael Scott Christofferson has persuasively argued, the same concern drove many former leftists in these years (including Furet and the *nouveaux philosophes*) to undertake a public campaign designed to portray the socialists (as well as the communists, their occasional allies) as crypto-totalitarian.[91] Foucault's somewhat more furtive intervention in this debate consisted in judging the Left from the standpoint of economic liberalism.

For if liberalism was the quintessential form of modern governmentality, it soon become clear that France's Left was hopelessly antiquated. To make this point, Foucault, in 1979, took the circuitous route of considering Ordoliberalism, the German economic school that theorized the Federal Republic's "social market economy." The school owes its name to the journal *Ordo*, founded in 1948 by a group of liberal economists who had met at the University of Freiburg before the war. Their finest hour came when they undertook a liberal critique of the economic policies pursued by Allied occupation authorities in the immediate postwar period. Soon, they found their way to the antechambers of finance minister Ludwig Erhard, the architect of West Germany's "economic miracle."[92] Despite the devastation in which Germany found itself in these years, the Ordoliberals did not back away from their liberal convictions – if anything, they became even more convinced that humanity's future depended on the renunciation of collectivism in all its forms. They were unsparing in their critique of Keynesianism; according to Foucault, Wilhelm Röpke, one of their most prominent members, went so far as to dismiss the Beveridge Report, which paved the way for Britain's National Health Service, as warmed-over National Socialism.[93]

Though firmly committed to the capitalist economy, the Ordoliberals were not, however, crude free-marketeers. Their beliefs boil down to a single crucial insight: everything that neoclassical economics says about the free market's virtues is true; the problem, however, is that competition is a quasi-mathematical ideal, not an empirical reality. For competition to work its magic, it must first be jump-started by the state. Specifically, the state needs a robust legal framework, one that allows marketplace competition to approximate its ideal form (though like the utilitarians, it should be noted, the Ordoliberals conceived of law as a political tool, not as the state's metaphysical foundation). What seems to have intrigued Foucault about Ordoliberalism is that it confirmed his intuition that economic liberalism should be thought of as a political and not merely an economic system. As Foucault put it, it is precisely Ordoliberalism's insistence that intervention in the economy be limited (such as refraining from economic planning and price-setting) that requires intervention in the legal realm – that is, the legislation and jurisprudence that will grease the market's gears. Trying not to govern too much, it turns out, keeps a government rather busy.

Moreover, because they believed that a free market required an efficient state, the Ordoliberals were also responsible for a remarkable political transformation: the historic decision of the German Social Democratic Party (SPD) to renounce Marxism at its 1959 Bad Godesberg conference. Foucault cautioned against denouncing the Bad Godesberg decision as a betrayal. In the first place, by 1959, the SPD needed to embrace neoliberalism and renounce its commitment to mass nationalizations to be a serious contender in electoral politics. But second, and more importantly, the Bad Godesberg decision endowed the SPD with a program for governing. As Foucault put it, the conference marks the SPD's entry into "the game of governmentality."[94]

Critical lessons were thus to be gleaned from the German experience. The SPD had reconciled itself with liberalism and then, a decade later, rode to power with Willy Brandt. Yet in June 1977, François Mitterrand could declare, "There is no way out for liberal society, [either] we will defeat it, or it will defeat itself" – before losing elections (once again) the following year.[95] As Foucault saw it, the most pernicious problem with Mitterrand and his supporters was not their leftist orientation, but their inability to recognize socialism's constitutive shortcoming: the fact that there is "no autonomous socialist governmentality."[96] Historically, Foucault argued, socialists come to power brimming with ideas, but invariably find themselves borrowing governmental practices – the means by which they actually get things done – from other political traditions: from economic liberalism, for instance, in the case of the German SPD, or from the police state, in the case of Soviet socialism. Socialism is deficient in this way because socialists have always been more enamored of texts than of practices: they become consumed, for instance, by the problem of authenticity – that is, with the question of what "true" socialism really is – in ways that often privilege fidelity to foundational texts over political and administrative know-how (this political critique is, interestingly, analogous to a philosophical one that Foucault had leveled against Jacques Derrida[97]). What the SPD had learned from Ordoliberalism, but which still escaped the French Left, was not how to love capitalism, but how to govern. Those on the Left who believed that power matters would thus be wise, he suggested, to learn more about liberalism.

Foucault's critique of French socialism resonated with contemporary arguments advanced by the Second Left. The lecture in which Foucault made his remarks on French socialism was delivered shortly before the Socialist Party's Metz conference, during which Rocard and his supporters publicly questioned the wisdom of the party's commitment to a "rupture with capitalism." These efforts were, in the end, fruitless: the platform ultimately adopted by the socialists denounced the "so-called 'economic laws' that are presented on the Right as eternal, analogous to those of cosmology."[98] Foucault's frustration with French socialists endured, even after they finally came to power in 1981. Didier Eribon recounts, for instance, how in 1983 he and Foucault had planned to publish a short book entitled *La Tête des socialistes* [*The Socialist Mindset*], which would have demonstrated that socialism is bereft of an "art of governing"[99] – the conclusion that Foucault had first reached in 1979. Their broadside against socialism never made it to print. Even so, one imagines that, by 1983, Foucault felt vindicated by the course of events: faced with a deteriorating economic climate, Mitterrand's government suspended its ambitious program of nationalizations, devalued the franc, and adopted austerity measures that de facto acknowledged the market's laws – a Bad Godesberg moment, yet an unacknowledged one, sowing confusion from which the party has never quite recovered.

Claiming that socialism's political relevance required that it come to terms with economic liberalism was daring enough. But Foucault, in 1979, upped the ante: far from inaugurating a new form of fascism, as some leftist intellectuals were suggesting, neoliberalism, he maintained, should be seen as a distinctly nondisciplinary form of power. To make his case, he turned to the Chicago School. No doubt surprising his listeners with his sudden interest in economic policy, Foucault explained the provisions of the so-called "negative tax," an idea explored in the early 1960s by the Chicago economist Milton Friedman (a guru of the Thatcher and Reagan revolutions), which had also sparked interest in France when the liberal economist Lionel Stoléru endorsed it in a noted essay published in 1974.[100] The negative tax seeks to streamline costly social-service bureaucracies and to eliminate work disincentives created by certain welfare programs. With the negative tax, the government no longer worries about guaranteeing that only the deserving poor receive assistance. The sole criterion for defining poverty, and the only level at which the state intervenes to reduce it, is income. Rich and poor alike file tax returns; however, those whose income falls below a particular threshold receive a cash handout inversely proportional to their means, rather than paying a portion of their income in taxes. What intrigued Foucault about this idea (enacted in the United States as the "earned income tax credit" in 1975, and in France as "le prime pour l'emploi" in 2001) is that it broke with the tendency of the modern welfare state to link payouts to behavior. Eliminating the long-standing distinction between the "good" and the "bad" poor, the negative tax is supremely indifferent to the spending choices and work habits of its recipients. What matters is solely that they be guaranteed an income that allows them to be players in the economic game.[101] All of which suggests, Foucault maintained, that capitalism has entered a new era. Compared to the *dirigiste* policies of the postwar years, neo-liberalism of the Chicago variety is "much less bureaucratic," and "much less disciplinary" (*disciplinariste*)[102] – which, coming from Foucault, was no mean compliment.

American neoliberalism's nondisciplinary implications were perhaps even more apparent in its approach to a question that had long been one of Foucault's deepest concerns: that of crime and punishment. For neoliberalism jettisons the oppressive moral categories characteristic of discourses on crime. The Chicago economist Gary Becker, for instance, demonstrates that, to understand criminal behavior, there is no need to define crime as anything more than any individual action that incurs the risk of punishment. The criteria of good and evil, normal and abnormal, and even of legal and illegal can be happily dispensed with. Discussing models that explain how market mechanisms might regulate drug use more effectively than law enforcement, Foucault marvels that, with these approaches, the criminal undergoes an "anthropological erasure."[103] Furthermore, rather than nursing the fantasy of a crime-proof society, the Chicago School advises that it is more useful for a society to calculate how much crime and punishment it can afford. In his concluding remarks about the Chicago School, Foucault presents neoliberalism as an almost providential alternative to the repressive disciplinary model of society:

> what appears [in American neoliberalism] is not at all the ideal or the project of an exhaustively disciplinary society in which the legal network encircling individuals would be relayed and prolonged from within by mechanisms that are, let us say, normative. Nor is it a society in which the mechanism of general normalization and of the exclusion of the

non-normalizable would be required. One has, on the contrary...the image or the idea or a programmatic theme of a society in which there would be an optimization of the system of differences, in which the field would be open to oscillating processes, in which there would be a tolerance accorded to individuals and to minority practices, and in which not the players of the game, but the rules of the game would be acted upon, and at last in which there would not be an intervention of the kind that internally subjugates individuals, but an intervention of the environmental kind.[104]

Openness to "differences," "tolerance" of individuals and minority practices, restraint in the practice of subjugation: these are not words that we customarily associate with Foucault's vision of political modernity. That he used them in 1979 to describe the course of power relations in modern societies reveals just how much his understanding of politics had evolved since the publication of *Discipline and Punish* four years earlier.

Conclusion

Foucault's 1979 lectures, I have argued, should be read as a strategic endorsement of economic liberalism. Three reasons explain his decision. In the first place, the intellectual, political, and economic factors that contributed to the rehabilitation of economic liberalism in France during the 1970s allowed Foucault to recognize its affinities with his nonjuridical theory of power. In the process, he ultimately revised the hypothesis of *Discipline and Punish*, arguing, rather, that the paradigmatic form of modern power is not discipline, which governs individuals by regulating their bodies, but the far less intrusive technique of population management that he dubbed biopower. Because biopower requires the state to step back and defer to spontaneous human interaction (even if it recognizes that the state must occasionally nudge these forces in particular directions), it paves the way for economic liberalism. Second, while many intellectuals were weaning themselves off Marxism through a newfound admiration for political liberalism, Foucault, who remained constitutionally allergic to that philosophy's humanistic underpinnings, turned instead to economic liberalism – precisely because he appreciated the thinness of its anthropological claims. Third, Foucault believed that the chief problem of the contemporary French Left was its inability to make the leap from ideology to governmentality: only by reconciling itself with neoliberalism, he contended, could it endow itself with the tools needed to wield power.

What emerges from Foucault's lectures on economic liberalism is, then, a different Foucault – at the very least, one considerably at odds with the Foucault that has been so vehemently debated by the American academy. Rather than a philosopher who explores the marginalized and excluded in order to challenge the pretenses of dominant epistemological and discursive systems, we find a Foucault intrigued with the ways in which a particular discursive framework – one that at the time was aspiring to hegemony – might accommodate difference and minority practices. As I have argued, we risk being tone deaf to this Foucault when we fail to grasp the context in which his words were uttered. Indeed, the shift in Foucault's thought from "discipline" (into which one might incorporate, in addition to his 1975 work, his studies of the 1960s) to "biopower" (as exemplified by economic liberalism) corresponds in many respects to a broader transformation in French society: from the full-employment, *dirigiste* model of the postwar era to the globalized – and precarious – order born in the 1970s. Hence the danger of too readily pinning on Foucault those labels that American conventional wisdom uses to identify him – "postmodernism," "post-structuralism," or "French theory." These terms are not, of course, devoid of content: insofar as they refer, in Foucault's case, to his philosophical antihumanism, his suspicion of anthropological claims, and his nonjuridical conception of power, they have their use. But too often, these labels have become associated with forms of academic discourse and politics that, amongst other shortcomings, are almost constitutively incapable of articulating why a thinker whom their adherents hail as pathbreaking could find himself, in the late 1970s, impressed with a way of thinking destined to become as closely tied to the prevailing global order as economic liberalism. As Foucault scholasticism and postmodernism's more vulgar iterations slowly lose their purchase, the time has perhaps come to situate Foucault's true significance in the deeper historical shifts to which his thought testifies, rather than the intellectual rebellion that he is presumed to have led.

Notes

This chapter originally appeared in *Modern Intellectual History* 6, 3 (2009). It is reprinted with permission from Cambridge University Press.

1 See J. Sawicki, *Disciplining Foucault: Feminism, Power, and the Body* (New York: Routledge, 1991); M. A. McLaren, *Feminism, Foucault, and Embodied Subjectivity* (Albany: SUNY Press, 2002); and L. McNay, *Foucault and Feminism: Power, Gender, and the Self* (Boston, MA: Northeastern University Press, 1993).

2 D. M. Halperin, *Saint Foucault: Towards a Gay Hagiography* (New York: Oxford University Press, 1995), 120. On Foucault and queer theory, see also J. Butler, *Gender Trouble: Feminism and the Subversion of Identity* (New York: Routledge, 1990); and T. Spargo, *Foucault and Queer Theory* (Duxford and New York: Totem, 1999).

3 A. L. Stoler, *Race and the Education of Desire: Foucault's History of Sexuality and the Colonial Order of Things* (Durham: Durham University Press, 1995), 1. See also E. Said, *Orientalism* (New York: Vintage Books, 1978); and R. Guha and G. Chakravorty Spivak, eds., *Selected Subaltern Studies* (New York: Oxford University Press, 1988), especially the section entitled "Developing Foucault."

4 See P. O'Brien, "Michel Foucault's History of Culture," in L. Hunt, ed., *The New Cultural History* (Berkeley: University of California Press, 1989), 25–46; and J. Goldstein, ed., *Foucault and the Writing of History* (Oxford and Cambridge: Blackwell, 1994).

5 The foundational text of governmentality studies is G. Burchell, C. Gordon, and P. Miller, eds., *The Foucault Effect: Studies in Governmentality* (Chicago: University of Chicago Press, 1991).

6 *The History of the Present*, edited by Paul Rabinow of the University of California at Berkeley, appeared between 1985 and 1988. The online journal *Foucault Studies*, founded in 2004, is available at www.foucault-studies.com.

7 C. Paglia, "Junk Bonds and Corporate Raiders: Academe in the Hour of the Wolf," in Paglia, *Sex, Art, and American Culture* (New York: Vintage Books, 1992), 224.

8 M. Foucault, "Qu'est-ce que la critique? (Critique et Auflklärung)," *Bulletin de la société francaise de philosophie* 84, 2 (1990): 38.

9 J. Habermas, "Modernity versus Postmodernity," trans. S. Ben-Habib, *New German Critique* 22 (1981): 13.

10 J.-P. Sartre, "Jean-Paul Sartre répond," *L'Arc* 30 (1966): 88.

11 M. S. Christofferson, *French Intellectuals against the Left: The Anti-Totalitarian Moment of the 1970s* (New York: Berghahn Books, 2004). See also J. Bourg, *From Revolution to Ethics: May 1968 and Contemporary French Thought* (Montreal and Ithaca: McGill-Queen's University Press, 2007); and A. Jainchill and S. Moyn, "French Democracy between Totalitarianism and Solidarity: Pierre Rosanvallon and Revisionist Historiography," *Journal of Modern History* 76 (2004): 107–54.

12 By "economic liberalism," I mean the school of thought that holds the free market to be the most efficient of economic systems. Though in practice they are often related, I distinguish it from "political liberalism," understood as the philosophy that advocates representative governments grounded in law and guaranteeing fundamental human rights. "Neoliberalism" will refer, as it does for Foucault, to the twentieth-century forms of economic liberalism associated with German Ordoliberalism and the Chicago School.

13 Foucault, "Entretien avec Madeleine Chapsal," in Foucault, *Dits et écrits*, vol. I, *1954–1969*, ed. D. Defert, F. Ewald, and J. Lagrange (Paris: Gallimard, 1994), 516.

14 Foucault, "Foucault répond à Sartre" (interview with J.-P. Elkabbach), in *Dits et écrits*, vol. I, *1954–1969*, 664.

15 M. Walzer, "The Politics of Michel Foucault," *Dissent* 30 (Fall 1983): 490.

16 R. Wolin, "From the 'Death of Man' to Human Rights: The Paradigm Change in French Intellectual Life, 1968–1986," in Wolin, *The Frankfurt School Revisited, and Other Essays on Politics and Society* (New York: Routledge, 2006), 180. For a similar argument, see F. Dosse, *Histoire du structuralisme*, vol. II, *Le chant du cygnet: 1967 à nos jours* (Paris: La Découverte / Livre de poches, 1992), 392–4.

17 E. Paras, *Foucault 2.0: Beyond Power and Knowledge* (New York: Other Press, 2006), 97.

18 R. Rorty, "Moral Identity and Private Autonomy: The Case of Foucault," in Rorty, *Essays on Heidegger and Others* (Cambridge and New York: Cambridge University Press, 1991).

19 J. Rajchman, *Michel Foucault: The Freedom of Philosophy* (New York: Columbia University Press, 1985), 123.

20 J. Colombel, *Michel Foucault. La clarté de la mort* (Paris: Odile Jacob, 1994), 210.

21 F. Lebaron, "De la critique de l'économie à l'action syndicale," in D. Eribon, ed., *L'infréquentable Michel Foucault. Renouveaux de la pensée critique. Actes du colloque Centre Georges-Pompidou, 21–22 juin 2000* (Paris: EPEL, 2001), 163.

22 J. Revel, *Expériences de la pensée. Michel Foucault* (Paris: Bordas, 2005). Revel maintains (unpersuasively, in my view) that Foucault distinguished between "biopower," the political technology associated with economic liberalism, and "biopolitics," the means through which biopower is resisted.

23 Foucault, *La volonté de savoir* (Paris: Gallimard, 1977), 117.

24 Those who would see Foucault's interest in liberalism and his turn, in the early 1980s, to subjectivity as qualifications or even rejections of his earlier antihumanism overlook the fact that Foucault considered both projects to be examinations of "governmentality," a concept whereby he endeavored to replace the juridical model of power and its humanist underpinnings with a conception of power as a practice and as a relationship through which subjects are constituted. Thus, in 1981, Foucault claimed that his "history of subjectivity" was part and parcel of the "question of "governmentality,"" insofar as the "government of the self by oneself " raises the issue of its "articulation in relation to others": Foucault, "Subjectivité et vérité," in Foucault, *Dits et écrits*, vol. IV, *1980–1988*, ed. D. Defert, F. Ewald, and J. Lagrange (Paris: Gallimard, 1994), 214.

25 It is, however, worth recalling that Foucault had studied the works of Adam Smith and David Ricardo in *The Order of Things*, albeit from an epistemological rather than a political perspective.

26 Foucault, "Entretien avec Michel Foucault" (interviewed by D Trombadori in 1978), in Foucault, *Dits et écrits*, vol. IV, *1980–1988*, 80, 81.

27 Quoted in D. Macey, *The Lives of Michel Foucault* (New York, 1993), 348.

28 See Foucault, "La grande Colère des faits" (a review of André Glucksmann's *The Master Thinkers*), in Foucault, *Dits et écrits*, vol. III, *1976–1979*, ed. D. Defert, F. Ewald, and J. Lagrange (Paris: Gallimard, 1994), 277–81; reproduced, in translation, as chapter 8 in this volume.

29 J. A. Frieden, *Global Capitalism: Its Fall and Rise in the Twentieth Century* (New York: W. W. Norton, 2006), 359.

30 See, for instance, M. Parodi, *L'économie et la société française depuis 1945* (Paris: Armand Colin, 1981), 12–61.

31 J. Fourastié, *Les Trente glorieuses, ou la révolution invisible de 1946 à 1975* (Paris: Fayard, 1979).

32 See J.-J. Becker and P. Ory, *Crises et alternances (1974–2000)* (Paris: Seuil, 2002), 63–74.

33 J. Fourastié, "La fin des temps faciles," *Le Figaro*, December 20, 1973, 1, 26.

34 J. Rueff, "La fin de l'ère keynésienne," in *Oeuvres complètes de Jacques Rueff*, vol. III, *Politique économique I* (Paris: Plon, 1979), 178. This article, originally a lecture delivered to the Mont Pèlerin Society, appeared in *Le Monde* on February 19 and 20–21 1976.

35 F. A. von Hayek, *Scientisme et sciences sociales: essai sur le mauvais usage de la raison*, trans. Raymond Barre (Paris: Plon, 1953).

36 Becker and Ory, *Crises et alternances*, 78–81.

37 A. Fourçans, "France: la politique du gouvernement Barre et le néo-libéralisme," in *Universalia 1979: les événements, les hommes, les problèmes en 1978* (Paris: Encyclopaedia Universalis France, 1979), 279.

38 T. B. Smith, *France in Crisis: Welfare, Inequality, and Globalization since 1980* (Cambridge and New York: Cambridge University Press, 2004), 91–4.

39 See, respectively, M. Fourcade-Gourinchas and S. L. Babb, "The Rebirth of the Liberal Creed: Paths to Neoliberalism in Four Countries," *American Journal of Sociology* 108, 3 (2002): 562–8; and M. Prasad, "Why Is France so French? Culture, Institutions, and Neoliberalism, 1974–1981," *American Journal of Sociology* 111, 2 (2005): 366, 370.

40 Fourcade-Gourinchas and Babb, "Rebirth of the Liberal Creed," 564.

41 Prasad, "Why Is France so French?" 366.

42 P. Drouin, "La France est-elle libérale?" *Le Monde*, October 7, 1978, 32.

43 For instance, the Walter Lippmann Colloquium, which met in Paris in 1938, has recently attracted the attention of scholars, who have identified it as a foundational moment of modern neoliberalism. See S. Audier, *Le Colloque Lippmann. Aux origines du néo-libéralisme* (Latresne: Bord de l'eau, 2008); and F. Denord, "Aux origines du néo-libéralisme en France: Louis Rougier et le Colloque Walter Lippmann de 1938," *Le Mouvement social* 195 (2001): 9–34.

44 Prasad, "Why Is France so French?" 375.

45 J.-F. Kesler, quoted in *ibid.*, 375. See the volume that Rosa coedited with F. Aftalion, *L'économique retrouvée. Vieilles critiques et nouvelles analyses* (Paris: Economica, 1977).

46 Prasad, "Why Is France so French?" 375.

47 See, for instance, G. Elgozy, *Le bourgeois socialiste, ou pour un post-libéralisme* (Paris: Calmann-Lévy, 1977); P. Malaud, *La révolution libérale* (Paris, New York, Barcelona, and Milan: Masson,

1976); and A. Sauvy, *La tragédie du pouvoir. Quel avenir pour la France?* (Paris: Calmann-Lévy, 1978).

48 F. A. Hayek, *Prix et production* (Paris, 1975); Hayek, *Droit, législation et liberté. Une nouvelle formulation des principes libéraux de justice et d'économie politique*, trans. Raoul Audouin (Paris: Presses universitaires de France, 1980); Hayek, *Le mirage de la justice sociale*, trans. Raoul Audouin (Paris: Presses universitaires de France, 1981); M. Friedman, *Inflation et systèmes monétaires*, revised edn, trans. D. Caroll (Paris: Calmann-Lévy, 1977); Friedman, *Contre Galbraith* (Paris: Economica, 1977); M. Friedman and R. Friedman, *La liberté du choix*, trans. G. Casaril (Paris: P. Belfond, 1980).

49 Hayek, "L"hygiène de la démocratie," *Liberté économique et progrès social. Périodique d'information et de liaison des libéraux* 40 (1980–1): 20–37.

50 M. Foucault, *Naissance de la biopolitique. Cours au Collège de France, 1978–1979* (Paris: Seuil/Gallimard, 2004), 221.

51 On this issue, see W. Gallois, "Against Capitalism? French Theory and the Economy after 1945," in J. Bourg, ed., *After the Deluge: New Perspectives on the Intellectual and Cultural History of Postwar France* (Lanham, MD: Lexington, 2004), 49–72. This chapter seeks to qualify Gallois's claim that Foucault partook in French theory's neglect of economic thought.

52 H. Lepage, *Demain le capitalisme* (Paris: Hachette, 1978), 11.

53 *Ibid.*, 13; original emphasis. A similar argument was made by F.-P. Bénoît in *Démocratie libérale* (Paris: Presses universitaires de France, 1978).

54 Lepage, *Demain le capitalisme*, 422.

55 E. Maire and J. Julliard, *La CFDT aujourd'hui* (Paris: Seuil, 1975), 185.

56 P. Rosanvallon, *L'age de l'autogestion* (Paris: Seuil, 1976), 45.

57 Lepage, *Demain le capitalisme*, 420–1.

58 J. Baechler, "Libéralisme et autogestion," *Commentaire* 1 (1978): 32. Rosanvallon replied to Baechler's complaint, to which he was clearly sensitive, in "Formation et désintégration de la galaxie "auto," " in P. Dumouchel and J.-P. Dupuy, eds., *L'auto-organisation. De la physique au politique* (Paris: Seuil, 1983), 456–65. I am grateful to Sam Moyn for sharing these references.

59 Rosanvallon, *L'age de l'autogestion*, 41–5.

60 H. Lepage, *Autogestion et capitalisme. Réponses à l'anti-économie* (Paris: Masson, 1978).

61 Unpublished letter from Foucault to Rosanvallon, dated Dec. 17, 1977. This letter was kindly made available to me by Sam Moyn. See also Rosanvallon, "Un intellectuel en politique" (interview with Sylvain Bourmeau), available at www.college-de-france.fr/

media/his_pol/UPL57428_Un_Intellectuel_en_politique.pdf. This interview originally appeared in *Les Inrockuptibles* 566 (Oct. 3, 2006).

62 Foucault, "Une mobilisation culturelle," *Le Nouvel Observateur* 670 (Sept. 1977), 49. Foucault would subsequently collaborate with the CFDT on a number of issues, including opposition to the repression of the Polish trade union Solidarity in 1981 and efforts to rethink the French social security system. For the latter, see R. Bono, B. Brunhes, M. Foucault, R. Lenoir, and P. Rosanvallon, *Sécurité sociale. L'enjeu* (Paris: Syros, 1983). Foucault's archives testify to further projects. See notably a letter on CFDT stationery from Alexandre Bihous, addressed to – in addition to Foucault – Pierre Bourdieu, Jacques Julliard, Claude Lefort, Kryztof Pomian, Pierre Rosanvallon, Paul Thibaud, Alain Touraine, and Patrick Viveret, entitled "Propositions de travail commun intellectuel – Confédération française démocratique du travail": Fonds Foucault, Institut mémoires de l'édition contemporaine (IMEC) (Saint-Germain-la-Blanche-Herbe, France), FCL 6.11.

63 P. Rosanvallon, "L"état en état d'urgence," *Le Nouvel Observateur* 670 (Sept. 1977), 49, 48.

64 Rosanvallon, *La crise de l'état-providence* (Paris: Seuil, 1992; first published 1981), 97.

65 Foucault, *Discipline and Punish: The Birth of the Prison*, trans. A. Sheridan (New York: Vintage, 1977; first published 1975), 296. The original passage is in the interrogative form.

66 *Ibid.*, 308. In his translation, Sheridan makes this footnote the book's final paragraph.

67 James Miller points out, on Daniel Defert's testimony, that Foucault started writing what became the final chapter of the first volume of *The History of Sexuality* – "The Right of Death and Power over Life" – on the very day that he completed *Discipline and Punish*. This suggests that Foucault's reservations about the scope of the "disciplinary hypothesis" may date back as far as 1975. See Miller, *The Passion of Michel Foucault* (New York: Simon & Schuster, 1993), 240–1.

68 Foucault, *"Il faut défendre la Société." Cours au Collège de France, 1975–1976* (Paris: Seuil/Gallimard, 1997), 215.

69 *Ibid.*

70 *Ibid.*, 216, 218–19.

71 *Ibid.*, 220.

72 *Ibid.*, 216.

73 *Ibid.*, 223–4.

74 Foucault, *Sécurité, territoire, population. Cours au Collège de France, 1977–1978* (Paris: Seuil/Gallimard, 2004), 47.

75 Foucault, *Discipline and Punish*, 206.

76 *Ibid.*, 202–3.

77 Foucault, *Sécurité, territoire, population*, 50.

78 See Miller's *The Passion of Michel Foucault*, as well as J. Seigel, *The Idea of the Self: Thought and Experience in Western Europe since the Seventeenth Century* (New York: Cambridge University Press, 2005), 603–31.

79 Foucault, *Sécurité, territoire, population*, 68.

80 Foucault, *Naissance de la biopolitique*, 23, 24. Foucault uses the term *libéralisme*, not "economic liberalism," but clearly means the latter, and not liberalism's political form. In the opening lecture, for instance, he speaks in one breath of "liberalism, of the Physiocrats, of Adam Smith, of Bentham, of the British utilitarians" (*ibid.*, 25). I use the term "economic liberalism" in the interest of clarity.

81 *Ibid.*, 323.

82 *Ibid.*, 325.

83 *Ibid.*, 25.

84 Rosanvallon had close ties to Furet as well as to Foucault.

85 Foucault, *Naissance de la biopolitique*, 41.

86 Though Furet, too, was critical of many aspects of revolutionary politics, it was ultimately the Revolution's failure to ground political life in a solid legal framework, rather than its rootedness in such a tradition, that he condemned.

87 Foucault, *Naissance de la biopolitique*, 43.

88 *Ibid.*, 324.

89 Quoted in Fourçans, "La politique du gouvernement Barre," 279.

90 For these reasons, Maria Bonnafous-Boucher's argument is exactly wrong: Foucault does not embrace what she calls "liberalism without liberty," but rather liberty without liberalism – at least insofar as the latter is understood in a more conventional (i.e. humanistic) sense. See Bonnafous-Boucher, *Le libéralisme dans la pensée de Michel Foucault. Un libéralisme sans liberté* (Paris: L'Harmattan, 2001).

91 Christofferson, *French Intellectuals against the Left*.

92 See Jean François-Poncet, *La politique économique de l'Allemagne occidentale* (Paris: Sirey, 1970); and H. Rieter and M. Schmolz, "The Ideas of German Ordoliberalism, 1938–1945: Pointing the Way to a New Economic Order," *European Journal of the History of Economic Thought* 1, 1 (1993): 87–114.

93 Foucault, *Naissance de la biopolitique*, 114. Foucault's editors, however, find no evidence that Röpke ever makes precisely this claim. See 131, n. 39.

94 *Ibid.*, 92.

95 Quoted in J. Moreau, "Le Congrès d'Epinay-sur-Seine du Parti socialiste," *Vingtième Siècle* 65 (2000): 95.

96 Foucault, *Naissance de la biopolitique*, 93.

97 Foucault, "Mon corps, ce papier, ce feu," in Foucault, *Dits et écrits*, vol. II, *1970–1975*, ed. D. Defert, F. Ewald, and J. Lagrange (Paris: Gallimard, 1994), esp. 267–8.

98 Quoted in Moreau, "Le Congrès d'Epinay," 95.

99 D. Eribon, *Michel Foucault* (Paris: Flammarion, 1991), 325–6.

100 L. Stoléru, *Vaincre la pauvreté dans les pays riches* (Paris: Flammarion, 1974).

101 Foucault, *Naissance de la biopolitique*, 210–11.

102 *Ibid.*, 213.

103 *Ibid.*, 264.

104 *Ibid.*, 265.

3

Foucault, the Excluded, and the Neoliberal Erosion of the State

Daniel Zamora

In a conference in Tokyo in April 1978, Michel Foucault wondered whether we were not witnessing, "in the late 20th century, something that would be the end of the age of the Revolution."[1] This Foucauldian "end of the revolution" does not, however, resemble that of François Furet, but rather "a proliferation of struggles aimed at redistributing the game of power in society."[2] In the eyes of Foucault, this transformation parallels the decline of Marxism and the contemporary problems to which it led. Foucault, in this way, builds on the conclusions he had reached in *The Order of Things*: that Marxism was perfectly integrated into nineteenth-century thought, but that it was far less relevant to grasping the late twentieth century. In our own day, it would seem that our attention is only focused on the margins of employment, as we dwell on prisoners, the mentally ill, sexual minorities, and other marginalized groups. While Foucault had always been interested in issues related to groups that are "excluded" from modern forms of employment and the traditional processes of labor commodification, this issue became politically significant only in the second half of the 1970s. This period experienced not only a proliferation of political initiatives benefitting the "Lumpenproletariat," but also efforts to challenge the centrality of work, the working class, and traditional means available to it for securing rights (parties, unions, social security[3]). A broad conception of identity thus came to replace the problem of exploitation. As the concept of "social class" disappeared from philosophical analysis, the struggle against capitalism was gradually being replaced by a struggle against normalization of behaviors and identities imposed on subjects, as well as against Marxism and "social Statism."

The "last" Foucault of the early 1980s is surprising in his thinly veiled sympathy for, and minimal criticism of, emerging neoliberalism. While a "great transformation" was being prepared ideologically as well as politically, Foucault, far from having anticipated the future consequences of these shifts, almost encouraged them in the name of greater autonomy and the subject's rebellion against major institutional structures and "grand narratives."

This transformation is important because, in a few years, it would replace a conception of social justice based on reducing inequalities with a vision that strove primarily for equal opportunities and the fight against "exclusion." Although Foucault cannot be held responsible for events that he did not witness, it seems legitimate to ponder the "last Foucault's" political implications.

In search of a "new plebeian"

The economic crisis in Western economies at the turn of the 1970s and the movement of May 1968 had significant impact on intellectual debates and social contestation. In addition to being a movement of large-scale strikes, May 1968 helped to foreground a wide array of "specific" struggles, such as sexuality, "everyday life," and racism. As for the economic crisis, it would ultimately deliver a fatal blow to the labor movement by drastically shrinking the workforce and its social and symbolic power due to the emergence of mass unemployment. This context gave birth to several important theoretical trends.

In the intellectual realm, the new form of capitalism brought about by mass unemployment led many authors, as Slavoj Žižek puts it, to redefine "social agents who could play the role of the revolutionary subject, as understudies who might replace an indisposed working class: Third World peasants, students, intellectuals, the excluded."[4]

Among these authors, Marxist theorist Herbert Marcuse was particularly outspoken in defending the idea that the traditional working class had become "integrated" into the capitalist system and that only "active minorities" and "the young middle-class intelligentsia" were capable of radical political action.[5] According to Marcuse, these "underprivileged" groups, which were, at least on a symbolic level, "humiliated, frustrated, oppressed, victims of segregation,"[6] had allied themselves with students, a key factor in triggering the 1960s revolts. The epicenter of the "social earthquake" was thus no longer to be found in the traditional proletariat, but rather in the "unemployed," "black ghettos," the "poor and suffering," and other marginalized "ethnic" groups. These arguments culminated in the work of André Gorz, who, beginning in 1980, defended the idea that the traditional worker had disappeared and, with it, the idea of a class that was "able to take charge of the socialist project and translate it into reality."[7] In his view, "the majority of the population now belong to the post-industrial neo-proletariat which, with no job security or definite class identity, fills the area of probationary, contracted, casual, temporary and part-time employment."[8] Unlike the Marxian "proletariat," this new social group would no longer be defined by its position in the social process of production, but by the fact that it lacked any sense of being a class – as well as by its "exclusion" from society, the basis of its purported radicalism. Many variations of this basic claim would be advanced by leftist intellectuals in the 1970s.

Even if Foucault was relatively removed from these debates within Marxism, he nevertheless seems to have been rather taken with the new theoretical and practical appeal of the "underclass" (*sous-prolétariat*). For him, as for many authors of the time, these new figures seemed politically important, even constituting a new vector of social contestation. In his eyes,

Political parties tend to ignore these social movements and even weaken their strength. From this point of view, the importance of all these movements is clear to me. All these movements occur among intellectuals, among students, among prisoners in what is called the *Lumpenproletariat*. Not that I recognize an absolute value to their movement, but I still believe it is possible, in terms of both logic and policy, to recover what has been monopolized by Marxism and the Marxist parties.[9]

The question thus became how to overcome the apathy of a working class that had been rendered passive due to the rights it had acquired and its acceptance of bourgeois ideology. Foucault did not hesitate to stress that, due to "the way the proletariat was repressed in the nineteenth century," at present, "various political rights have been granted," meaning that "the bourgeoisie obtained the promise from the proletariat of good political conduct and the renunciation of open rebellion."[10] Consequently, the proletariat had "internalized part of the bourgeois ideology"[11] – an ideology "of order, virtue, acceptance of laws, what is and is not suitable."[12] Its spirit, however, which harks back to "the use of violence, insurgency, crime," is now found in "the underclass, [at] the margins of society."[13] For Foucault, the solution to working-class apathy thus lay in the need for these "violent marginal strata of the plebeian population [to] regain their political consciousness. For example, these youth gangs in the suburbs, in some parts of Paris, for whom their state of delinquency and their marginal existence take on political significance."[14] This excluded population was thus the spark needed to rekindle the aspirations of the gentrified proletariat. Indeed, only through a "fusion" of these groups could a "mass movement" driven by the revolt of "marginalized plebs" occur.[15]

These views were perfectly consistent with the types of action Foucault undertook in collaboration with the Proletarian Left (Gauche prolétarienne). Indeed, during his Maoist period, when he often interacted with Pierre Victor,[16] he drew closer to the Maoists' political approach. Actions such as the occupation of buildings for the homeless, the distribution of food to African immigrants, and demonstrations for the rights of prisoners echoed his own political ideas. This shift of the locus of political action from the working class to more "marginal" groups would lead Sartre to speak of essentially "moral gestures" and the emergence of a "moral Marxism."[17]

Its moral dimension lay in its concern with "minorities," "marginals," and the "excluded," and thus with the issue of domination and discrimination. These new struggles fell within what Foucault called, in 1972, "an entirely new phenomenon, which is related to the appearance of the new plebeians"[18] who constitute the "non-proletarianized" faction of the working class.

As the working class has slowly lost its central place in social struggles, along with the universality it purportedly embodied – which brought many intellectuals into politics – there emerged a need to find alternative struggles intellectuals could support. In this context, the intellectual's role was no longer to invoke grand narratives and universal principles, as Sartre had once done, but rather to "speak of all kinds of experiences, listen to the needs of the aphasic, the excluded, the dying...I [Foucault said] think the job of a philosopher living in the West is to listen to these voices."[19] For philosophers at that time, the main question was to understand how part of the population was excluded, rather than how the majority was exploited.[20] The problem is not, needless to say, that a range of previously ignored forms of domination have now been recognized, but the fact that they are increasingly theorized independently of any notion of exploitation. Far from drawing a theoretical perspective that examined the relationship between exclusion and exploitation, Foucault gradually saw them as opposed, and even as contradictory.

From the redistribution of wealth to the redistribution of power

Foucault would partially pursue this orientation in his late work of the early 1980s. Gradually abandoning the prospect of revolution as well as class-based social analysis, he focused his research on the concept of "governmentality" and the resistance it generates. The agent of this resistance no longer has any clear economic basis, but is defined, rather, by the position it occupies in relation to various forms of power. Thus, although he distanced himself considerably from the radical thought of his Maoist period, the fact remains that his attention was still focused on minority figures who existed independently from relations of exploitation. In his view, poverty and economic inequality were essentially a nineteenth-century problem. While he readily conceded that these issues were not entirely resolved, they no longer need to be addressed "with the same urgency."[21]

Thus, according to Foucault, if "the nineteenth century is concerned primarily with relations between the major economic structures and the state apparatus," at present it was micropowers and "diffuse systems of domination" that "have become the fundamental problems."[22] The problem of exploitation and wealth would be replaced by one of excessive power,[23] focused on controlling the conduits and modern forms of pastoral power. He calls this "specific frame of resistance to forms of power" "revolts of conduct."[24] Foucault is referring not to the "Lumpenproletariat," or any social classes at all, but to the excluded, and struggles relating to sexual liberation and the effects of knowledge in realms as diverse as medicine, social security, and crime.

These specific struggles that Foucault describes in his 1978 course at the College de France[25] are primarily directed against the forms of governmentality that exist in our society. This theme is thus a natural extension of Foucault's long-standing interest in social institutions and, in particular, in the ways in which they standardize conduct. His work and observations led him to be struck

> by the attention that the state brings to bear on individuals; one is struck by all the techniques that have been established and developed so that the individual in no way escapes either authority, or supervision, or control, or the wise, or training, or correction. All major disciplinary machinery – barracks, schools, workshops and prisons – are machines that permit the identification of the individual, know who he is, what he does, what we can do, where to place him, how to place him among the others.[26]

To all these institutions, Foucault is careful to add "mechanisms of assistance and insurance," because "in addition to their goals of economic rationalization and political stabilization," "they make life and existence possible for everyone, but they also define each person as a separate event that is relevant, that is even necessary and indispensable to the exercise of power in modern societies."[27] True to his intellectual trajectory, Foucault conceived of social security as a tool that standardizes conduct and individuals. As he remarked in 1983, "our systems of social security impose a particular way of life to which individuals are subjected, and any person or group that, for one reason or another, will not or cannot embrace that way of life is marginalized by the very operation of the institutions."[28] It is therefore important to reinvent, disclose, and shed light on the "relations that exist between the functioning of social security and lifestyles."[29] Studies on governmentality will therefore be the starting point for Foucault and some of his followers, such as François Ewald, to problematize the centrality of the welfare state to "modern forms of power."[30]

It is interesting to note that in Ewald's main book, which was not only dedicated to Foucault but largely prepared under the latter's direction, he does not hesitate to write that "the welfare state fulfills the dream of 'biopower.' The welfare state is a state that is intended not so much to protect individual freedom against the aggressions it may undergo from others as to support the very way that the individual manages his life."[31] He added that "if the welfare state, like the liberal state, focused on the economy, it is no longer an economy of material wealth, but an economy of life."[32] Thus, Ewald, like Foucault, does not see the welfare state simply as an extension of earlier forms of disciplinary power, but rather as an entirely new system. Foucault observes: "this stance of pervasive concern is the present status of the state. It is that mode of power that then develops."[33] Anxiety arising from uncertainty and the lack of security is the foundation upon which allegiance to the state and its categories is based, which involves accepting "everything, taxes, hierarchy, obedience, because the state protects and guarantees against insecurity."[34]

Yet even as they operate under this reassuring cover, these institutions seek to perpetuate power, to watch us "day by day,"[35] and to normalize the behavior and identities they shape. It is these identities, which were created by a modern state that has incorporated "pastoral Christian power as a life management tool,"[36] that became the crucial issue in

Foucault's eyes. In this spirit, he writes, "since the 1960s, subjectivity, identity, and individuality constitute a major political problem,"[37] and so our priority must become "our subjectivity, our relationship to ourselves."[38] At the dawn of the 1980s, it seemed clear to Foucault that the redistribution of wealth had ceased to be a pressing concern. He did not hesitate to write that "one could say that we need an economy that does not relate to the production and distribution of wealth, but an economy that would focus on power relations."[39] What mattered was not so much power, "in the form of economic exploitation,"[40] but resistance to everyday forms of power, as one sees with feminism, student movements, prisoners, undocumented immigrants, etc. This "struggle against power in everyday life"[41] is ultimately about "refusing" power. This movement obviously has implications for the political goals it advocates and its increasingly pronounced refusal of socialist and communist strategies. For Foucault, "the goal of all these movements is not the same as the traditional political or revolutionary movements: it is absolutely not about targeting political power or economic systems."[42] Gone are the "big state and institutional battles"; we must now fight for the "destabilization of mechanisms of power" and reject all forms that aim to standardize behaviors and the identities of individuals. As he wrote, "that kind of resistance and struggle has as its goal the facts of power themselves, much more than something like economic exploitation, much more than something like inequality. What is at stake in these struggles is that a power is exercised, and that the mere fact that it is exercised is actually intolerable."[43] Although Foucault does not take an essentially normative view of these developments that unfold before him, he seems nevertheless convinced that these movements have actually superseded an outdated struggle against exploitation.

Fighting exclusion, not inequality

This idea of an "end" to the struggle against exploitation and inequality, in favor of greater emphasis on the redistribution of power, is echoed by many organizations that fight on behalf of the "excluded" to gain recognition of this new political agency's "specificity" and ensure its "participation" in the political process. These actors and political movements are increasingly focused on the idea that there lie, at wage labor's margins, a growing number of people who are excluded from the welfare state and dominant systems of labor. Of central importance to these groups is the non-governmental organization ATD Fourth World (ATD quart monde),[44] which, since the mid-1960s, has widely disseminated the idea of an underclass relegated to the margins of dominant labor systems. This organization identifies a "people without identity or public life,"[45] who deserve the right to exist politically. This new issue shifts the traditional theoretical goalposts by asking: "how is it that throughout history we encounter situations in which the disadvantaged are not exploited by others, but, rather, are expelled from society as such?"[46]

It is interesting to note how close these questions are to those Foucault poses when defending the idea that we should, above all, "provide a critique of the system that explains the process by which modern society marginalizes part of the population."[47] Both ATD and the "last" Foucault believe that "transforming the production system or the ownership of means of production does not, on its own, lead to more equal freedom and opportunity for all. This does not change conditions for the poorest part of the population, unless a minimum of human rights are simultaneously introduced that allow it to move out of exclusion."[48] Basically, traditional policies of solidarity seek only to "reshuffle the deck between those who are already playing the game,"[49] rather than addressing the excluded. The heart of the problem is the fact that this social group, which finds itself "locked in the straitjacket of exclusion" and is reduced to "an ignored population, always rallying, but continually disbanding,"[50] has no capacity to represent itself and no identity. These people, excluded from "workers' solidarity" and social security,[51] are in "a specific collective situation,"[52] which requires equally specific measures if the question of redistribution is to be addressed. This issue is not only political, but also symbolic, as it seeks to recognize, through a very precise conceptual arsenal, the existence of new social groups that no longer fit into the traditional class grid. By its political and symbolic existence alone, this supposedly new player profoundly disrupts the Left's traditional political concerns. It transforms not only established tools for fighting inequality, but also the very concepts of inequality and social justice. Due to this emphasis on the fragmentation of the working class and the importance it assumes in public debates, "social exclusion" will have lasting political effects. Indeed, inequality in a general sense will cease to be considered the problem; rather, emphasis will be placed on the form it takes for specific social categories. Thus, although one can reasonably assume that this was never the intention of any specific author, we cannot overlook the effects of the approaches they advocated, given that their analyses have proved relevant to the processes that divide inequality's effects, rather than those that generate inequality itself. The 1970s, however, witnessed a proliferation of books and essays adopting this oppositional attitude and reconfiguring social assumptions underpinning social policies of the postwar era. Consider René Lenoir's book *Les exclus. Un Français sur dix* [*The Excluded: One Frenchman Out of Ten*]: it calls attention to social misfits, the physically and mentally handicapped, people with psychosomatic diseases, drug addicts, neurotics, and criminals, and notes that "the marginal fringe is expanding."[53] In a volume edited with Michel Foucault, Lenoir also attacked the idea that inequality remained the primary social problem. From his perspective, reducing inequality is "unrealistic"[54] and would not seriously change the condition of the "excluded." The many books and essays of this kind have, however, generally fared poorly on the political Left.[55] Take the example of Jean-Michel Belorgey, a former socialist member of parliament who is seen as the founder of the Revenu minimum d'insertion (RMI, a form of minimum wage), who did not hesitate to declare in 1988 that "the concepts of poverty, exclusion, and social marginality have never been successful on the Left."[56] He explains that leftist thinkers "have, over the years, never stopped seeing the ideological weapons of the Right as hiding the phenomenon of the exploitation of workers, and the capitalist economic system's responsibility for this."[57] Thus, although he, too, later defended the creation of a specific and targeted policy parallel to the social security system for the "poor" and other "excluded" populations, he nevertheless acknowledged that such an approach "is not without drawbacks, in that it is likely to endorse the exclusion of normal forms of solidarity for a large fraction of the marginalized sectors of society."[58] Yet this fear that he describes so well seems, far from having been avoided, to have been realized, as the "political struggle against exclusion" or "against poverty" has replaced political struggles against inequality, the extension of social security, and the preservation of labor law. As Colette Bec remarked, this slow political construction of an excluded "people" "helped provide a theoretical basis...for the separation of the social question from the production process."[59] The end of the fight against inequality through social security, and the call for another system, thus paved the way for the neoliberal assault on the welfare state and social security systems for means-tested and limited welfare.

The neoliberal erosion of the state

On these issues, Foucault's analysis was not limited to the issue of the exclusion of the marginalized from social security and the forms of domination it reproduces; he also seems to have endorsed very liberal positions on these topics, at the very moment they had begun to emerge in France. This trend found support among what is now known as the French "Second Left," a minor but influential current in French socialism associated with Michel Rocard's Unified Socialist Party (Parti socialiste unifié, or PSU) and the French Democratic Confederation of Labor (Confederation française démocratique du travailleur; CFDT), a major union. Other figures involved in this movement include Pierre Rosanvallon, whose work Foucault appreciated for its anti-statism and its ambition to "de-stateify French society."[60] At the time, Foucault summed up relatively faithfully the emerging view that social security's "increasing rigidity"[61] would have a negative impact on economic vitality, entrepreneurship, and so on. Without adopting any critical distance from it, Foucault cited a 1976 report published in the *Revue française des affaires sociales*, which maintained that social security raised the costs of labor excessively, and was partly responsible for unemployment.[62] On health-care spending, Foucault's opinion was even more clear, and close to the neoliberal view. Far from unconditionally supporting the basic idea of the system, he harshly criticized it. Though health-care needs are not quantifiable and limited, he observed, it is "not possible to lay down objectively a theoretical, practical threshold, valid for all, on the basis of which it might be said that health needs are entirely and definitively satisfied."[63] This conclusion, which reproduced classic arguments used by opponents of public health-care systems, led him to the conclusion that it is "clear that there is little sense in speaking of the 'right to health.'"[64] He then asked the question of whether a society must "try to satisfy by collective means individuals' need for health?" "And can those individuals legitimately claim satisfaction of those needs?"[65] And he continues, declaring that "a positive answer to this question could take no acceptable or even conceivable form."[66]

Foucault's rhetorical move is closely related to free-market liberal arguments against universal health-care systems, which is based on the premise that a universal "right" to health can be objectively determined for the entire population. This view has been gradually repudiated, in favor of the idea, which Hayek defended, that health care is a consumer good like any other, and that it is each individual's responsibility to "choose" whether to purchase care or not. Thus, A. W. Gaffney notes that, for Hayek, "one person might prefer paying rent to having a mammogram, while another might take a needed heart surgery over a week on vacation." As a result, "the idea that there is an 'objectively' determinable standard of medical services which can and ought to be provided for all, a conception which underlies the Beveridge scheme and the whole British National Health Service, has no relation to reality."[67] In this sense, Hayek, just like Foucault, "disputes the very notion that there could exist anything like a universal desire – much less a 'right' – to any social good, including health care."[68]

Although Foucault takes care to immediately clarify that he's "not advocating, it goes without saying, any kind of wild liberalism that would lead to individual coverage for those with means and an absence of cover for the rest,"[69] it seems to him nonetheless quite clear that "it would in any case be impossible to allow expenditure on health to increase at the rate seen in recent years."[70] In a text from 1976, he also invokes the classic neoliberal argument that welfare (specifically health care) ultimately amounts to a subsidy that the poor pay to the rich, as it is the rich who benefit most from the various services welfare provides. Foucault says: "social transfers that we had hoped for from social security systems do not work as expected.... The rich continue to use medical services much more than the poor. This is true in France today. The result is that small consumers, who are also the poorest, pay for the over-consumption of the rich."[71] This argument, widely popularized by Milton Friedman in *Free to Choose* – which presumably would not have escaped Foucault's attention – objects as a matter of principle to any universal publicly financed service, as such systems lead, according to Friedman, to "transfer[s] from the less well-off to the better-off."[72] Needless to say, Friedman's argument essentially encourages private systems. Finally, Foucault also indicates that social security, "whatever positive effects it has" – although he never explicitly states them – also has "perverse effects," such as the maintenance of certain mechanisms of "dependence."[73] Situated at the crossroads between a neoliberal critique and a sixties-era critique, emphasizing emancipation and empowerment rather than assistance, Foucault argues that "what one ought to be able to expect from security is that it gives each individual autonomy in relation to the dangers and situations likely to lower his status or subject him."[74] He thus advocates greater "participation" on the part of users, encouraging each to take greater responsibility for their choices.[75] While it is, of course, always difficult to make a retrospective analysis, his heavy-handed discourse is rather tendentious.

Foucault's critique of bureaucracy and views about accountability, efficiency, and cost management, with all their ambiguities, lead some to see him as a precursor to Third-Way Blairism. Moreover, as José Luis Moreno Pestaña notes, "there remains in the 'last' Foucault much of the leftist cultural critique and a program close to a liberal social democracy – which admits capitalism as an inevitable reality, considering that the state can only produce more bureaucracy, and the welfare state, far from being a condition of true citizenship, submerges the individual in relationships of dependence."[76] Colin Gordon, a leading translator of and commentator on Foucault in the English-speaking world, does not hesitate to declare that "parts of the formulae of Clinton and Blair for a 'third way' may have effectively carried out a form of the operation which Foucault might have been taken as challenging the socialists to contemplate – the selective incorporation, in an updated and corrected social democracy, of certain elements of neoliberal analysis and strategy."[77]

Although Foucault never clarified what the proper form of socialist governmentality should be, it is interesting to note that he remained attracted to an alternative to welfare state principles proposed by Milton Friedman in 1962 in his famous book *Capitalism and Freedom*, as well as in 1980's *Free to Choose*:[78] specifically, the negative income tax. This is a formula that has been widely adopted in various forms since the 1980s by the liberal "new Left" under the idea of the basic income.[79]

Neoliberalism and the negative tax as emancipation

Given the many defects of the traditional social security system, Foucault seemed interested in the idea of a negative income tax. The idea is relatively simple: the state provides a benefit to anyone below a certain income threshold. There is no question of differentiating between the employed or the unemployed, the deserving or the undeserving poor; everyone whose income is beneath a certain level receives some payment from the government. The goal is to ensure, without major administrative costs, that no one will find themselves below a particular minimum level. For Milton Friedman, of course, these measures are intended to spell the end of public services. From his perspective, it is preferable to subsidize individuals directly than to pay for public services.

This debate appears in France as early as 1974 through the work of Lionel Stoléru, *Vaincre la pauvreté dans les pays riches* [Overcoming Poverty in Rich Countries]. To fight against poverty, Stoléru advocates a radical reform of social security, which he compares to an inefficient colander. His work makes two main arguments. First, this system would directly address the effects of poverty (by providing allocations), rather than inefficiently dealing with its causes (i.e. determining who among the poor are or not deserving). Next, along the same lines as Milton Friedman, he endorses a basic philosophical argument that distinguishes between a policy that seeks equality (socialism) and a policy that simply sets out to eliminate poverty, without challenging other economic inequalities (liberalism). For Stoléru, "doctrines...can encourage either a policy to eradicate poverty or a policy seeking to limit the gap between rich and poor."[80] This involves what he calls the "the border between absolute poverty and relative poverty."[81] The former simply refers to an arbitrarily determined level (addressed by the negative tax), while the latter relates to broader differences between individuals (addressed by social security and the welfare state). As Stoléru sees it, "the market economy is able to assimilate actions against absolute poverty" but "it is unable to digest strong remedies against relative poverty."[82] This is why he argues that "the distinction between absolute poverty and relative poverty is actually the distinction between capitalism and socialism."[83] The challenge of shifting from one to the other is ultimately a political question: namely, accepting or rejecting capitalism as the dominant economic system.

Foucault seems to have been very drawn to Stoléru's argument. He devotes a long passage of *The Birth of Biopolitics* to it. Although it veers subtly back and forth, as Pestaña notes, "between analysis and positive evaluations,"[84] the passage on negative tax seems relatively positive in tone. It is precisely the non-selective basis upon which it is granted that seems to have appealed to him. This system, it would seem, struck him as an answer to governmentality and the normalization of conduct imposed by old statists and centralized institutions. As he notes, the system goes beyond

> the famous distinction that Western governmentality has tried for so long to establish between the good and bad poor, between the voluntary and involuntary unemployed...After all, it does not and should not concern us to know why someone falls below the level of the social game; whether he is a drug addict or voluntarily unemployed is not important. Whatever the reasons, the only problem is whether he is above or below the threshold.[85]

The new system will allow assistance of the "floating" or surplus population, with respect to the labor market, "in a very liberal and much less bureaucratic and disciplinary way than...by a system focused on full employment which employs mechanisms like those of social security."[86] Thanks to a mechanism that rejects any distinction between the different groups of the "poor," "it is up to people to work if they want or not work if they don't. Above all there is the possibility of not forcing them to work if there is no interest in doing so. They are merely guaranteed the possibility of minimal existence at a given level, and in this way the neoliberal policy can be got to work."[87] In this way, we avoid basically everything Foucault criticized for years in the course of his work – all those ways of controlling the body, conduct, and sexuality that are so present, despite being hidden, in many socialist policies aimed at reducing inequality. One can feel a certain sympathy in Foucault for "the virtues of the anthropological economism of neoliberalism."[88] As Pestaña points out, Foucault believed that "neoliberalism does not project its models onto the individual: they have no performative effect and do not project any form of normality; they are only part of a framework of comprehensibility for understanding the behavior of the subject."[89] *Homo economicus* is an agent to whom only rational calculations are of interest. His choices are not judged from a moral point of view, but understood solely on the basis of interests. After all, it is not for the state to decide what individuals should do with their money (i.e. spend it on health, education, consumer goods, etc.). They alone should be able to decide, without being subject to normative judgments. Thus, neoliberalism finally makes "individuals...responsible for their lives without imposing a defined anthropological model.... Individuals do not have to submit to any rule concerning how to live, to love or to have fun; they simply have to ensure subjective and objective means to get there."[90] Although we can understand his enthusiasm for the idea of establishing a universal system, his interpretation has, of course, been totally contradicted by history. Not only have injunctions to work increased with the advent of Workfare, but also the great homogenization of conduct and lifestyles generated by neoliberal rationality has hardly emancipated individuals from normativity.

Finally, on the question of passing from a policy aimed at reducing inequalities toward a simple fight against poverty, Foucault's position remains vague. Although it is clear to him that "this negative tax is a way of absolutely avoiding social policy having any kind of effect in the form of a general redistribution of income,"[91] and therefore is "the exact opposite of socialist policy,"[92] it is still relatively difficult to determine his views on the matter. He could not, however, ignore the challenge that Stoléru had formulated so clearly in his book. The shift from one policy to another followed necessarily from the idea that "if we reach the top incomes, then we affect the heart of the dynamism of the market economy and its ability to invest, create, and select investments." Doing this would be to "remove from the competitive economy both the compass that directs it and the mechanism that drives it, and thus to give the control of our destiny to the state. Leaving the fate of the economy to the state is what I call socialism."[93] What was at stake in the debate in which Foucault found himself was thus the choice between acceptance of capitalism on the one hand, and socialism and reducing inequalities on the other. In defining, to use Ewald's terms, his age as "fundamentally post-revolutionary,"[94] the last Foucault seems to have made his choice.

Conclusion

Foucault's intellectual trajectory is unique in many respects: not only in its richness, but also in the way he was constantly evolving and able to conceptualize, and even anticipate, the problems of his time. He seems to always embody – while distancing himself from – the spirit of his age. Whether as a member of the French Communist Party, during his Gaullist period, or when he moved toward the Maoist movements, he was always in very productive dialogue with his own political beliefs. As a kind of "fellow traveler," not in a party but in a time that found itself in intellectual turmoil, Foucault was always one step ahead of his contemporaries. Even so, the "last" Foucault's thinly veiled sympathy for, and minimal criticism of, the emerging neoliberal paradigm is surprising. Also, while a "great transformation" was coming, far from

having anticipated its future consequences, he almost encouraged it in the name of greater autonomy and the subject's
rebellion against major institutional structures and entrenched
discourse. From this point of view, Foucault was no stranger
to the rejection, over the preceding 30 years, of debates about
inequality, alternatives to capitalism, and the political and
institutional tools needed to fight it. The intellectual consecration of neoliberalism by the Left as well as the Right, and the
"symbolic coup" after which one principle of vision and division of the world (one of social classes and exploitation) has
been superseded by another (one of exclusion and poverty[95]),
are integral parts of Foucault's (and many others') intellectual
development. Therefore, the strategy chosen by much of the
Left in the 1970s, during which its discourse began to address
the "fragments" of wage labor and denounce "the state" and
the "centralist conception of social transformation,"[96] seems
to have resulted in a twofold defeat, with the Right winning
economically as well as ideologically. The Right won economically because the decline of forms of "socialist" intervention and state regulation have not led to greater autonomy
and individual freedom; and it prevailed ideologically because
the idea that we must fight the effects of inequality (exclusion,
poverty, urban marginality, etc.) has ceased to be focused on
achieving equality, and has settled for creating more equality
of opportunity.

   In the end, identity politics and "revolts of conduct" bolstered a deeply humanitarian struggle for "respect," "integration," and a "life of dignity," yet at the expense of a much
less "moral" struggle for redistributing wealth. As Stephano
Azzara puts it, "the victory of neoliberalism can be measured
by the degree to which it has been able – sometimes explicitly
but more often without anyone realizing it – to penetrate and
restructure the vision of its opponents."[97] Thus, far from
having triumphed over its enemy in a duel to the death, neoliberalism has often converted its enemies unwittingly to its
own ideas. The story of what François Cusset called "the
greatest nightmare of the 1980s" is thus more complicated
than it seems, having seeped its way into our society's remot-
est corners. It follows that it has now become essential to
reconstruct, intellectually and politically, an egalitarian
project, yet without renouncing the critique of all these

"nooks and crannies" that the Left has largely abandoned to the prevailing orthodoxy.

Notes

1 M. Foucault, "La philosophie analytique de la politique," June 1978, in Foucault, *Dits et écrits*, vol. II, *1976–1988* (Paris: Gallimard, 2001), 547.

2 M. C. Behrent, "Penser le XXe siècle avec Michel Foucault," *Revue d'Histoire Moderne et Contemporaine* 60, 4-4 bis (2013).

3 "Social security" is the translation of the French "Sécurité sociale." It has a more extensive meaning than the American "social security" and denotes a broad range of social benefits for the working population (health care, pensions, unemployment benefits).

4 S. Žižek, *First as Tragedy, then as Farce* (London: Verso, 2009), 89.

5 H. Marcuse, *An Essay on Liberation* (Boston: Beacon Press, 1969), 51.

6 F. Perroux and H. Marcuse, *François Perroux interroge Herbert Marcuse...qui répond* (Paris: Aubier, 1969), 196.

7 A. Gorz, *Farewell to the Working Class* (London: Pluto Press, 1982), 66.

8 *Ibid.*, 69.

9 M. Foucault, "Méthodologie pour la connaissance du monde: comment se débarrasser du marxisme," April 25, 1978, in Foucault, *Dits et écrits*, vol. II, *1976–1988* (Paris: Gallimard, 2001), 603.

10 M. Foucault, "Le grand enfermement," March 1972, in Foucault, *Dits et écrits*, vol. I, *1954–1975* (Paris: Gallimard, 2001), 1170–1.

11 *Ibid.*

12 *Ibid.*, 1171.

13 *Ibid.*

14 *Ibid.*

15 M. Foucault, "Sur la justice populaire: débat avec les maos," June 1972, in *Dits et écrits*, vol. I, *1954–1975*, 1223.

16 Pierre Victor was a pseudonym for Benny Lévy (1945–2003), a political activist and philosopher, who was a leading figure of the Gauche prolétarienne between 1968 and 1973.

17 J. Gerassi, *Talking with Sartre* (New Haven, CT: Yale University Press, 2009), 96.

18 Foucault, "Le grand enfermement," 1171.

19 Foucault, "Méthodologie pour la connaissance du monde," 616.

20 Foucault, "Le grand enfermement," 1171.

21 Foucault, "La philosophie analytique de la politique," 536.

22 M. Foucault, "Michel Foucault: les réponses du philosophe," November 1975 in *Dits et écrits*, vol. I, *1954–1975*, 1674.

23 Foucault, "La philosophie analytique de la politique," 536.

24 M. Foucault, *Security, Territory, Population: Lectures at the Collège de France, 1977–1978*, trans. G. Burchell (London: Palgrave, 2007), 264.

25 *Ibid.*

26 Foucault, "La philosophie analytique de la politique," 551.

27 *Ibid.*

28 M. Foucault, "Social Security," in Foucault and L. D. Kritzman, eds., *Politics, Philosophy, Culture: Interviews and Other Writings, 1977–1984* (New York: Routledge, 1988), 164–5.

29 *Ibid.*

30 M. C. Behrent, "Accidents Happen: François Ewald, the 'Antirevolutionary' Foucault, and the Intellectual Politics of the French Welfare State," *The Journal of Modern History* 82 (2010): 587.

31 F. Ewald, *L'état providence* (Paris: Grasset, 1986), 374–5.

32 *Ibid.*, 375.

33 M. Foucault, "Michel Foucault: la sécurité et l'état," November 1977, in Foucault, *Dits et écrits*, vol. II, *1976–1988*, 385.

34 *Ibid.*, 386.

35 *Ibid.*, 387.

36 J. L. Moreno Pestaña, *Foucault, la gauche et la politique* (Paris: Textuel: 2011), 98.

37 Foucault, "Foucault étudie la raison d'État," 1980, in Foucault, *Dits et écrits*, vol. II, *1976–1988*, 856.

38 *Ibid.*

39 Foucault, "La philosophie analytique de la politique," 536.

40 Foucault, *Security, Territory, Population*, 259.

41 M. Foucault, "Sexualité et politique," May 1978, in Foucault, *Dits et écrits*, vol. II, *1976–1988*, 529.

42 Foucault, "La philosophie analytique de la politique," 545.

43 *Ibid.*

44 See C. Bec, *La sécurité sociale. Une institution de la démocratie* (Paris: Gallimard/Nrf, 2014), and M. Messu, *La pauvreté cachée* (Paris: L'aube, 2003), 117–19.

45 Mouvement ATD quart monde, *Livre blanc. Le sous-prolétariat en Belgique* (Brussels: ATD quart monde, 1977), 6.

46 *Ibid.*, 4.

47 Foucault, "Le grand enfermement," 1171.

48 Mouvement ATD quart monde, *Livre blanc*, 28.

49 *Ibid.*

50 *Ibid.*, 6.

51 *Ibid.*, 7.
52 *Ibid.*, 22.
53 R. Lenoir, *Les exclus. Un Français sur dix* (Paris: Seuil, 1974), 7.
54 R. Bono, B. Brunhes, M. Foucault, R. Lenoir, and P. Rosanvallon, *Sécurité sociale. L'enjeu. Entretiens avec Robert Bono* (Paris: Syros, 1983), 73.
55 J.-M. Belorgey, *La gauche et les pauvres* (Paris: Syros, 1988).
56 *Ibid.*, 19.
57 *Ibid.*
58 *Ibid.*, 27.
59 Bec, *La sécurité sociale*, 256.
60 See, in detail, chapter 2 by M. C. Behrent in this book.
61 Foucault, "Social Security," 160.
62 M. Foucault, *The Birth of Biopolitics: Lectures at the Collège de France, 1978–1979*, trans. G. Burchell (London: Palgrave Macmillan, 2008), 199.
63 Foucault, "Social Security," 169.
64 *Ibid.*, 170.
65 *Ibid.*
66 *Ibid.*
67 A. W. Gaffney, "The Neoliberal Turn in American Health Care," *Jacobin*, available www.jacobinmag.com.
68 *Ibid.*
69 Foucault, "Social Security," 175.
70 *Ibid.*, 171.
71 M. Foucault, "Crise de la médecine ou crise de l'antimédecine?" in Foucault, *Dits et écrits*, vol. II, *1976–1988* (Paris: Gallimard, 2001), 56.
72 M. Friedman and R. Friedman, *Free to Choose: A Personal Statement* (New York: Harcourt Brace Jovanovich, 1980), 106.
73 Foucault, "Social Security," 160.
74 *Ibid.*
75 *Ibid.*, 173.
76 Pestaña, *Foucault*, 131.
77 J. Donzelot and C. Gordon, "Governing Liberal Societies – The Foucault Effect in the English-speaking World," *Foucault Studies 5* (January 2008): 52.
78 See Friedman and Friedman, *Free to Choose*, 97.
79 See, for example, P. Van Parijs, *Arguing for Basic Income: Ethical Foundations for a Radical Reform* (London: Verso, 1992).
80 L. Stoléru, *Vaincre la pauvreté dans les pays riches* (Paris: Flammarion, 1974), 237.
81 *Ibid.*, 286.
82 *Ibid.*, 287.

83 *Ibid.*

84 Pestaña, *Foucault*, 120.

85 Foucault, *The Birth of Biopolitics*, 204–5.

86 *Ibid.*, 207.

87 *Ibid.*

88 Pestaña, *Foucault*, 120.

89 *Ibid.*, 121.

90 *Ibid.*, 122.

91 Foucault, *The Birth of Biopolitics*, 205.

92 *Ibid.*

93 Stoléru, *Vaincre la pauvreté dans les pays riches*, 289.

94 F. Ewald, "Foucault et l'actualité," in D. Franche et al., *Au risque de Foucault* (Paris: Editions du Centre Pompidou, 1997), 207.

95 F. Panier, "Pour une historicisation de l'*exclusion*: les raisons sociales du succès d'un quasi-concept" (Louvain, 2004), unpublished text.

96 P. Rosanvallon, "L'état en état d'urgence," *Le Nouvel Observateur* 670 (September 1977), 48–9.

97 S. G. Azzara, *L'humanité commune* (Paris: Delga, 2011), 12.

4

Foucault, Ewald, Neoliberalism, and the Left

Mitchell Dean

This chapter is an extended version of a lecture given at the British Library on the thirtieth anniversary of Michel Foucault's death.[1] On such occasions, it is not unusual to reflect upon the legacy of the individual so honored. Thus, in the limited time allowed, I raised the question of one aspect of the legacy of Foucault, accepting his status as among the most influential figures in the human and social sciences today. That aspect concerned neoliberalism. I had been struck by and wished to explore the claim made by one of his closest and most influential followers, François Ewald, that Foucault's lectures of 1979[2] had issued an "apology of neoliberalism."

There are, of course, many other aspects of Foucault's legacy with respect to political ideas. Temporally framing those lectures was his engagement with the Iranian revolution. It would be worth revisiting this extensive engagement and his claims for the global potential of Islamism, and "political spirituality" more generally – even more so in light of recent events in Paris and elsewhere.[3] Yet I chose the theme of "neoliberalism." Why? After all, isn't it a somewhat nebulous term, most often used as one of abuse and disavowed by those who are accused of being its proponents? Isn't associating Foucault with neoliberalism simply a provocation or, worse still, a practice of "denunciation" which Foucault himself would have rejected?[4] As one who had taken some sustenance in Foucault's thought over many years, I certainly did not wish to revive a denunciatory mode of criticism. However, it appeared that this issue requires robust intellectual debate precisely because neoliberal forms of reason are so often wrapped up in the politics of the present: whether in relation to austerity measures in Europe, inequality in the United States and the United Kingdom, or the kinds of solutions proposed for global poverty and climate change. Yet, for a new generation of critical scholars, it seemed to me, Foucault remained both a precious resource and a thinker rooted in, but not entirely bound by, the considerations of his own present. Rather than a return to a politics of intellectual and political denunciation, asking the question of Foucault's own relation to neoliberalism is a way of extending our own participation in present problems and the tools we have to address them. In this sense, it is a Foucauldian thing to do. I thus offer my own small contribution, which considers firstly the received view of Foucault's governmentality lectures in light of Ewald's turn to neoliberalism, and secondly the arguments of Ewald himself, not forgetting that he has acted as Foucault's student, assistant, interlocutor, editor, and now the general editor of his lectures. I shall then move to Foucault's lectures themselves and some related texts. I conclude with some thoughts on moving beyond Foucault, or at least to a location that is necessarily somewhat different from his – advance sideways like the "crayfish" (*l'écrevisse*), as he put it.[5]

The case of Ewald and the received view of Foucault's governmentality lectures

On May 9, 2012, at the University of Chicago, François Ewald found himself in a seminar in the presence of Gary Becker, the Chicago economist whose work Foucault addressed in several lectures on *The Birth of Biopolitics* in 1979. Ewald described these lectures as the place "where he [i.e. Foucault – M. D.] made the apology of neoliberalism – especially the apology of Gary Becker, who is referred to...as the most radical representative of American neoliberalism."[6]

Ewald, it must be said, spoke here with some authority. He completed his doctorate on the welfare state [*l'État providence*] under Foucault, and he has the honor of being directly referred to in these lectures – coincidentally, precisely on the question of denunciation I just mentioned.[7] He would co-edit Foucault shorter pieces (*Dits et écrits*) and act as general editor for the recent publication of his lectures at the Collège de France. Yet he is something of a problematic figure for the Left: a "right Foucauldian" – as Antonio Negri put it[8] – who would promote what Maurizio Lazzarato describes as the "policies and mechanisms for...reconstructing society according to neoliberal principles" revealed to him in Foucault's lectures of 1979.[9] For Jacques Donzelot, a rival Foucauldian who also researched the history of social policy, Ewald's was "a classic case of counter-transference where the analyst falls blindly in love with his object."[10]

Indeed, Ewald had been a militant Maoist who would attempt to enlist Foucault in 1972 in what became known as L'Affaire Bruay – the rather dubious and dishonorable politics surrounding the still unsolved murder of the teenage daughter of a mining family in northern France, which included the public demand for the castration of the soon-to-be-released suspect who happened to work for the mining company as a lawyer.[11] He would nevertheless receive the Légion d'Honneur in 2006 for his services to the insurance industry and particularly to the employers' association, Medef, which included the break-up of corporatist arrangements between employers, unions, and the state, and the introduction of direct contractual negotiations, in what amounted to a self-styled "coup of civil society against the state" at the time of the premiership of Lionel Jospin.[12] While such a vision would appear to be a free-market libertarian version of the support of movements within civil society often attributed to Foucault,[13] it was consistent with Ewald's own position on the welfare state. For him, l'État providence had, paradoxically, marked the rise of society, not the state. The Medef move, then, was nothing more than the claim that the properly social dimension of the French welfare state had to be revivified. As Ewald explained at the time, the problem with the old way of doing things was that "politics had believed that it could legislate for the social"; in contrast, the *fondation sociale* (social restructuring) would "depoliticize the economy" through an "ethos of contract" and thereby be "a last chance for the organizations of employers and employees to be the organizers of civil society."[14]

Most critics of Ewald, however, would wish to position Foucault firmly on the Left, even as they point to Ewald's neoliberal political trajectory. They would have us believe that the student had fundamentally departed from his intellectual master. Negri, for instance, wrote of a "true Foucault" who follows Marx in the view that the "free market never existed, it has always been a mystification."[15] Colin Gordon has long positioned Foucault on the independent or "free" Left, and Michael Behrent has convincingly uncovered his relationship to the "Second Left" in France during the 1970s.[16] Behrent, however, stands out as one who is willing to contemplate the continuities between Foucault and Ewald.[17]

Moreover, sympathetic commentators on Foucault's lectures on neoliberalism in 1978–9, from Thomas Lemke[18] to Pierre Dardot and Christian Laval,[19] have argued that his approach to neoliberalism is far more radical than that of Marxism since it eschews the standard, reductive gestures of ideology critique that finds the processes of capital accumulation, and the material interests of capital or one of its fractions – such as finance capital – lurking behind its anti-statism and pro-individual-freedom claims. Following Foucault's call to "try to grasp the singularity" of neoliberalism,[20] they focus on his approach to neoliberalism as a "rationality" that "employs unprecedented techniques of power over conduct and subjectivities."[21] Lemke argues that in these lectures "the theoretical strength of the concept of governmentality consists of the fact that it construes neoliberalism not just as ideological rhetoric or as a political-economic reality, but above all as a political project that endeavours to create a social reality that it suggests already exists."[22] This political project "tries to render the social domain economic" and reduces welfare expenditure as it promotes individual responsibility and self-care. He draws the following conclusion with regard to Foucault's analysis: "This enables us to shed sharper light on the effects neo-liberal governmentality has in terms of (self)regulation and domination. These effects...are the product of a re-coding of social mechanisms of exploitation and domination on the basis of a new topography of the social domain."[23]

In brief, for these commentators, Foucault offers us a far more intellectually nuanced and politically nimble account of neoliberalism than does Marxism, but one that firmly originates – even if somewhat vaguely – on the Left. For all his intellectual authority, and biographical intimacy, Ewald fundamentally departs from Foucault in his embrace of neoliberalism. The master cannot be blamed for the sins of the followers.

But it is all too easy, I think, to draw these dividing lines between Foucault and neoliberalism, and Foucault and Ewald. What is at stake is more than how a famous Foucauldian scholar could undertake Ewald's political trajectory. It is a question about Foucault's own relation to neoliberalism and, even more fundamentally for us and for our present, the legacy of that relationship in contemporary thought and the human and social sciences. And just because we disagree with the political views of the star witness in understanding this relationship, it does not mean that we must reject his testimony *tout court*. Ewald's two encounters with Becker thus have the status – particularly after the recent death of the latter – of essential intellectual-historical documents that can, like all such documents, find corroboration or contradiction in other more or less authoritative sources, including and especially the lectures and interviews of Foucault himself.

Ewald meets Becker at the University of Chicago

In Chicago, Ewald would claim that Foucault offered an "apology *of* neoliberalism" and an "apology *of* Gary Becker." Allowing for language difficulties, perhaps he meant less "an apology *for*" than "an apologia *of*" neoliberalism and Becker – that is, Foucault offered a form of public defense of them, of their relevance, against those who would otherwise dismiss or denounce them. In fact, Ewald's appraisal of Foucault's relation to neoliberalism is even more positive than this. After discussing the post-1968 situation, he suggests Foucault answered the demand for a theory of the state with the notion of governmentality, within which economists would act as "truth-tellers" in relation to government. Foucault, he suggests, was searching for non-moral and non-juridical theory, and he found it in the economists. "That is the celebration of the economists' work, of your work," he said to Gary Becker.[24] Ewald counseled Becker that Foucault discovered in him the "possibility of thinking about power without discipline...your [i.e. Becker's] theory of regulation makes it possible to conduct the behaviour of the other without coercion, by incitation."[25] And there is no doubt that Ewald means all of this in an extremely complimentary way when he concludes this homage to Becker with respect to Foucault's views: "Certain kinds of truth-telling are death for liberty, other kinds of truth-telling give new possibilities for liberty. And he sees your work, your kind of analyses as creating the possibility to promote, to envision new kinds of liberty."

This is striking. But how should we read it – or hear it, as it was a spoken rather than written word, readily available in video form? Is Ewald merely using terms like "liberty" and "truth" in non-normative, value-neutral ways consistent with a general Foucauldian orientation? Or is he actively appreciative of the possibilities of Becker's approach to power and truth for forms of liberty? Doesn't the opposition between "death for liberty" and "new possibilities for liberty" clearly indicate an evaluative criterion at work here? And if he is saying that Foucault endorsed Becker's theory, then is this merely the reminiscence of one who projects his own current values and commitments retrospectively onto his former supervisor's words? Or is this a more or less accurate, more or less astute, interpretation of those words by one who not only was close to Foucault but also knew from direct experience the purposes of these analyses and who, in his editorial roles, continues to work closely with them?

At the end of this preliminary presentation of Foucault's interest in Becker, Ewald refers to Foucault's interest in the model of the economic agent contained in Becker's theory, and he goes further than the proposition that Foucault actively admired the latter's accomplishments. He claims that the idea of *Homo œconomicus* contained in Becker's theory was very close to what Foucault searched for with his theory of the subject and of subjectivity... And Foucault, with his theory of power, it was very difficult to think how the subject decides: he is decided by power relations. And maybe Foucault could find a solution in your work and maybe we can see the reading of your work by Foucault like a step between his earlier theory of power and the later Foucault lectures about subjectivity and so on.[26]

For Ewald, Becker – "the most radical of the American neoliberals," as Foucault called him[27] – was decisive in the transformation not only of Foucault's theory itself but also of the very movement of his thought from the analytics of modern forms of power to the analysis of ancient ethics and ascetics. In saying so, he corroborates the work of Andrew Dilts[28] who had already described Foucault's position on neoliberalism as one of "sympathetic critique and indebtedness" in making this very same intellectual shift.

We leave aside most of Bernard Harcourt's critical comments as moderator, not because they are without interest but because we are concerned here with the relation to neoliberalism of Foucault and those closest to him. We do note that Harcourt attempted to construct a critique of Becker's human capital theory by finding implied references to the dangers of a new kind of eugenics in Foucault's lectures. This has received an explicit rejection by Colin Gordon on the grounds of its lack of textual support.[29] We also shall put aside most of Becker's extremely pleased response to Ewald's statement of "Foucault's apology." However, there is something rather telling in this early exchange between Harcourt and Becker, in which Harcourt in a sense stands as a surrogate for many loyal Foucauldians:

> **Bernard Harcourt:** As a teaser for this seminar I will tell you that in a glorious email that Professor Becker sent to me the day before yesterday, Gary Becker wrote (referring to Michel Foucault's work), "I like most of it, and I don't agree with much..."
> **Gary Becker:** I don't *disagree* with much.
> **Bernard Harcourt:** "I don't *disagree* with much." Did I just say that? Is that Freudian perhaps? I will slow down and

repeat that! "I like most of it, and I do *not disagree* with
much. I also cannot tell whether Foucault is disagreeing with
me." That truly sets the tone for this historic conversation.[30]

We wonder what indeed "sets the tone." Is it Becker's surprising endorsement of Foucault's view of his work? Or is it
Harcourt's slip? Perhaps we should not read too much into
a slip of the tongue, for fear of being accused of deep hermeneutics or psychoanalysis. Yet there is something symptomatic in a Foucauldian academic's desire to find a fundamental
disagreement between Foucault and this exemplary neoliberal
economist. Harcourt, in this sense, makes a slip for all who
would want to maintain the critical nature of Foucault's
engagement with neoliberalism when even the most attentive
reader would be hard-pressed to find the grounds for such a
critique and when a close follower of these lectures (Gordon)
finds little evidence of the kind of critique he supposes.

At the end of this first conversation, Ewald does venture
what amounts to a kind of criticism of Becker's key notion
of human capital when he suggests that it is vulnerable to the
charge that it is liable "to produce a vision of man that is
very impoverished."[31] That vision is a "poor behaviorism" in
which individual behavior can be modified by different kinds
of stimuli. This simply gives Becker the chance to proclaim
the richness of a vision of man based on choice.[32] Nevertheless this does start to map out some of the ground for future
discussion.

The second seminar in Chicago focuses on Becker's theory
of crime and punishment and the corresponding lecture by
Foucault on March 21, 1979. Again, it commences with
Ewald's laudation of Becker's theory on a number of points
he ascribes to Foucault: as a critique of governmentality,
which is a new kind of truth-telling outside of moral consid-
eration; as a liberation from past criminological and anthropological models of *Homo criminalis*; and finally as an
economic approach that creates limits to power and the
state.[33] Again, Becker fails to find a critique of his work in
Foucault.[34] In the course of the discussion the issue of Becker
and behaviorism is raised again, now by Harcourt, and reference is made to Foucault's mention of the techniques of the
behavioral psychology of B. F. Skinner.[35] Ewald, for the most

part, is silent and only weighs in to contradict Becker's supposition that Foucault was a socialist:

> **François Ewald:** Socialist, no! On the Left.
> **Gary Becker:** But well, what does Left mean? In terms of the role of the government, let's say that Left usually means bigger government.
> **François Ewald:** At this time, Foucault was in search of a new kind of governmentality. It was the research for a new possibility in politics that motivated his work on governmentality.[36]

If Becker is somewhat puzzled by what Foucault's critique of his work is meant to be by this stage, he now seems rightly bewildered at the use of the very term "Left." Ewald does not help matters when he sidesteps the question about political orientation to the role of government by the clear obfuscation entailed in invoking "governmentality." The discussion has moved into the frame of a polite conversation between friends, at least as far as Ewald and Becker are concerned – or even perhaps of the same "thought collective," to cite Philip Mirowski's exceedingly useful term.[37] Ewald concludes that Becker made possible a "positivist" and immanent "critique of governmentality that is internal to the system," but raises what he regards as a Kantian normative question.[38] This concerns both the use of deterrence as a tactic of punishment that uses human beings as means to another end, and the impossibility in Becker's terms of gaining the information necessary to make the calculus that such deterrence will be effective.

We should note that this interpretation of Foucault by Ewald was not new, even if its early incarnations were somewhat more muted. In an essay dated from the mid-1990s, for instance, Ewald concerned himself with the nature of "philosophical acts" and explained what he had learnt from Foucault about the present: "Foucault posited that our current situation [*actualité*] is very fundamentally post-revolutionary: if there was an event in the 1970s, it was the disappearance of the revolution."[39] In a nod to Francis Fukuyama's thesis, and an explicit reference to Alexandre Kojève, Ewald suggests that it "is clear that the end of revolution, and the end of History represent the same event: it is an event in our consciousness of time."[40] What is left only belongs to "the order of administration, of management." But this does not mean that the state assumes a central importance. Quite the contrary, for the end of revolution brings about the end of the philosophical relevance of the state, which is "no longer a philosophical concern...The stakes are with respect to power, and this is a totally different location, a totally different zone, a totally different type of reality."[41] Ewald brings a philosophical refinement to what he views as Foucault's radical anti-statism.

In Ewald's view, this situation does not portend a world without events. Rather, anything can emerge from it. It makes possible new "philosophical acts," or "events which have the value of acts concerning being."[42] What would a philosophical act look like, then, in the realm of a politics without revolution and with a philosophically non-relevant state, which has been reduced to the order of management and administration? It would seem to Ewald that Foucault found an exemplar in Becker's theory and in neoliberalism.

Within a few years of these statements, and guided by his understanding of Foucault's actuality for the present, Ewald would be able to join in relations of power on the side of the neo-liberalizing fraction of business in France and seek a fundamental restructuring to the corporatist welfare state. For the former Maoist militant, Foucault was less the theorist who extended politics to the domain of multiple local struggles and more one who diagnosed the vacuity of a politics around the couple "revolution/state." It was not the extension of politics but its limitation that Ewald would take from Foucault.

Ewald puts Foucault's normative understanding of neoliberalism on the table, but, prior to examining it, I want to make a brief excursus to discuss some of the empirical intellectual-historical problems of Foucault's governmentality lectures and their implications.

Empirical deficits in Foucault's governmentality lectures

Foucault's 1978 and 1979 lectures on governmentality and neoliberalism have proved to be fertile sources of inspiration for scholars and set many research agendas, including what is broadly called "governmentality studies." But they can only continue to do this on the condition that they are open to criticism. One of the strengths of the lectures is the narrative by which Foucault can brilliantly tie together disparate literatures: Machiavelli and the anti-Machiavellians, reason of state, the *Poliziewissenschaften*, the Scottish Enlightenment, mercantilism, the notion of the pastorate in Judaism and the early Church fathers, Aquinas, Rousseau, and many others, up to the German and American versions of neoliberalism. However, we must be clear that, from an intellectual-historical perspective, there is nothing inviolable about his readings of this literature. We can thus nominate a fairly random list of problem areas of Foucault's readings in the governmentality literature that have been more fully documented elsewhere:

1   The identification of Machiavelli's problematic – or that attributed to him by the anti-Machiavellians – as containing a developed conception of the state and territorial sovereignty contradicts the findings of the works of Foucault's contemporaries, J. G. A. Pocock and Quentin Skinner, as noted by Keith Tribe.[43] Contra Foucault, Machiavelli is less an exemplar of sovereign authority within a territorial domain than a continuation of the ancient problematic of an art of government to which his critics made a reactionary and religious response.

2   The failure to insert Thomas R. Malthus's principle of population in his account of the emergence of a modern problematics of population and security, which has ramifications for his understanding of classical political economy and for the liberal government of life more generally.[44]

3   Given these first two points, the meta-historical dichotomy between "the safety [*sûreté*] of the Prince and his territory" and "the security [*sécurité*] of the population and those who govern it" is empirically unsustainable.[45]

4   A fundamentally incorrect reading of Adam Smith's notion of the "invisible hand," which denies not only its theological and providentialist references but also repeats nostrums about the metaphor that are common to

contemporary neoliberalism, concerning the beneficial effects of "the market" and the impossibility of knowledge of the economy or political interventions in relation to it.[46]

5   The premature curtailment of the "theological genealogy" of the economy by passing over the more literal translation of Gregory of Nazianus's *oikonomia pyschon* as an "economy of souls," in favor of the word "conduct," which acts to deny the political and governmental implications of theological conceptions of the economy and government.[47]

6   An account of Ordoliberalism that omits a reflection on the notion of "order" itself, thus missing a key term that makes the neoliberal project thinkable in Ordoliberalism and in Hayek's evolutionary framework and notion of "spontaneous social order," derived from Adam Ferguson.[48] It also excises the theological reference of the Ordoliberals to medieval scholasticism and the extent to which the idea of a "natural order" became what Ralf Ptak calls a "quasi-religious Ordo talisman."[49]

None of these, or other problem areas, "invalidate" Foucault's project or "prove" he was fundamentally mistaken about his narrative of governmentality and the role of neoliberalism within it. They do, however, alert us to the need to suspect studies that treat Foucault's lectures as the Bible of the intellectual history of government, liberalism, and neoliberalism. Moreover, they are indicative of what are at least tendencies in his admittedly complex narrative. These include:

1   A tendency to systematically downplay the way sovereignty is a part of the juridical–political improvisation of modern government centered on the territorial state,[50] and a concomitant reduction of law to a technology of government.

2   A tendency to provide a kind of teleological account of the transformation of power in terms of the emergence of a government founded in the self-government of individuals and based on the "rationality of the governed."[51]

3   A dialectical structure of the narrative in which critical political reason faces and overcomes successive

"transcendent" obstacles exemplified by the Prince, the family, the cosmo-theological order, the State itself, and so on, in the pursuit of a rationality of government immanent to the governed themselves.[52]

4 A focus on the more benign aspects of liberal political reason, including neoliberalism, as an ethos of the critique of state reason, in which liberalism is presented, as Jörg Spieker[53] puts it, "in terms of moderation, limitation and restraint on the exercise of political power," neglecting "how liberalism might be implicated in forms of normalization, exclusion and violence."

5 A concentration on the explicit neoliberal governmental rationalities and their objectives rather than technologies and their modes of implementation and the struggles that surround them. As far as neoliberal policies are concerned, as Paul Patton[54] has argued, Foucault's lectures focus neither on the strategies of their introduction nor on the struggles and resistances they might provoke, and while this is understandable given their appearance before the elections of Margaret Thatcher and Ronald Reagan, "these lectures fall short of a critical analysis of neoliberal governmentality," even by Foucault's own standards.

Given the provisional nature of Foucault's lectures on governmentality, these empirical deficits and analytical tendencies can be acknowledged without endangering the enduring analytical frameworks that might be derived from them. This at least is the view many of us have adopted in the constitution of a field of governmentality studies.

Foucault on the neoliberal utopia

For researchers of governmentality, Ewald's interpretation of Foucault's lectures and their political trajectory is completely mistaken. I have already cited Thomas Lemke's summation of the superiority of Foucault's critical genealogy of neoliberalism over ideology critique, but such a view remains interpretive of the lectures rather than being explicitly stated in them. If we look for an explicit critique of neoliberalism, it is somewhat harder to find. The major critical point comes in the final lecture of *The Birth of Biopolitics*. It concerns the possibility of a relationship between neoliberalism and behavioral techniques of manipulation through adjusting stimuli in the environment (in fact this is related to the critical point raised by Ewald). Foucault pinpoints the "paradox" of *Homo œconomicus*. On the one hand, starting in the eighteenth century, "from the point of view of a theory of government, *homo œconomicus* is the person to be let alone."[55] Now, in Becker's definition, *Homo œconomicus*

> appears precisely as someone manageable, someone who responds systematically to systematic modifications artificially introduced into the environment. *Homo œconomicus* is someone who is eminently governable. From being the intangible partner of *laissez-faire*, *homo œconomicus* now becomes the correlate of a governmentality which will act on the environment and systematically modify its variables.[56]

When this was put to him in 2012, Becker can respond: "I mean, yes, if you have things under certainty, there's a certain deterministic aspect of behavior you can modify a lot. But within that broad spectrum, people have a variety of choices they can take."[57] Choice, for the neoliberal, would seem to be the caveat that dissolves the critical point of this observation. After all, is it not better to "nudge" people in the right direction than compel them to act in a certain way?

It is thus incorrect to say that Foucault offered a wholly uncritical account of neoliberalism. However, a keener appreciation of the significance of Foucault's reading of American neoliberalism is given at the end of the previous lecture after his long discussion of the theory of crime and punishment in Becker and other neoliberals. Because of his supposition that power is omnipresent, Foucault's problematic is not one that seeks a freedom from *all* sorts of power but rather an alternative to *particular kinds* of power and regulation. Foucault finds in American neoliberalism a rather precisely defined alternative to the other new kinds of power and regulation he had analyzed:

> you can see that what appears on the horizon of this kind of analysis is not at all the idea of a project of an exhaustively disciplinary society in which the legal network hemming in

individuals is taken over and extended internally by, let's say, normative mechanisms. Nor is it a society in which the mechanism of general normalization and the exclusion of those who cannot be normalized is needed.[58]

This statement directly addresses the governing of crime, but not *just* that. It can be read in terms of the movement of Foucault's thought through forms of power. What is envisaged by American neoliberalism, then, is a form of regulation that is not one of a *sovereign* power exercised through law, or of *disciplinary* society with its norms, or even of the general normalization of a *biopolitics* of the population. It is not one of the major forms of regulation discussed by Foucault prior to these lectures on governmentality in 1978 and 1979, and nor is it the framework of biopolitics still attributed to the 1979 lecture course (no doubt due to its rather misleading title). Rather, it is a new program and vision:

On the horizon of this analysis we see instead the image, idea, or theme-program of a society in which there is an optimization of systems of difference, in which the field is left open to fluctuating processes, in which minority individuals and practices are tolerated, in which action is brought to bear on the rules of the game rather than on the players, and finally in which there is an environmental type of intervention instead of the internal subjugation of individuals [de l'assujettisement interne des individus].[59]

We have seen that Foucault expresses reservations about the project of the manipulation of choice through environmental interventions of the behavioral type. These would seem simply to be the costs – in his language, the "dangers" – of a form of neoliberal regulation that he finds has certain benefits – or "potentials." Chief among these is that regulation no longer entails the internal "subjectification" (assujettisement) of the individual. We need to attend to the French phrase translated in English as "of the internal subjugation of individuals." Assujettisement has a specific dual meaning in Foucault's thought: it not only means subjection in the sense of "submission to" or "subjugation" but also entails the fabrication or production of subjectivity. This dual meaning is underlined by the adjective "internal" that emphasizes not the mere external forms of subjugation (as the equivalent of domination) but the internal forms of subjugation as "subjectification," as the fabrication of subjectivity through relations of power and knowledge. Thus, Foucault here distinguishes the neoliberal program from those forms of regulation and power, such as discipline, that subjugate individuals through the production of subjectivity – that is through tying individuals to the truth of their identity, e.g. the occasional criminal, the recidivist, the dangerous individual, the invert, etc. For Foucault, in this passage, neoliberalism does not subjectify in this sense. By not doing so, it opens up the space for tolerating minority individuals and practices and optimizing systems of differences.

Some commentators have refused to be surprised by these statements from Foucault. They place him in the liberal tradition.[60] Moreover, Alain Beaulieu[61] draws our attention to Foucault's discussion, prefacing his excursus on American neoliberalism, of Hayek and the liberal utopia:

> Some years ago Hayek said: We need a liberalism that is a living thought. Liberalism has always left it to the socialists to produce utopias, and socialism owes much of its vigor and historical dynamism to this utopian or utopia-creating activity. Well, liberalism also needs utopia. It is up to us to create liberal utopias, to think in a liberal mode, rather than presenting liberalism as a technical alternative for government.[62]

The question of voice is difficult here. I would resist the view that Foucault here advocates a normative liberal theory. However, he found in the environmental interventions shaping choice for the American neoliberals a liberal way of governing that was not only technical but, notwithstanding its costs, a kind of liberal utopia. It might not have been a utopia to which he could fully subscribe, but it was one that had certain features he could appreciate.

This does not mean that Foucault was or became a card-carrying neoliberal. But it does demonstrate that, like many progressive intellectuals of his period and later, he would look into the liberal and neoliberal political repertoire to find ways of renovating social-democratic or socialist politics and escaping its perceived fatal statism. We know well his famous statements concerning a socialist governmentality in 1979:

I do not think that there is an autonomous socialist governmentality. There is no governmental rationality of socialism.
In actual fact, and history has shown this, socialism can only
be implemented connected up to diverse types of governmentality. It has been connected up to liberal governmentality,
and then socialism and its forms of rationality function as
counterweights, as a corrective, and a palliative to internal
dangers...We have seen it function, and still see it function,
within governmentalities that would no doubt fall more under
what last year we called the police state, that is to say, a hyper-
administrative state in which there is, so to speak, a fusion, a
continuity, the constitution of a sort of massive bloc between
governmentality and administration.[63]

What is of note here is not simply the rejection of the possibility of an independent socialist governmentality, but that
that alternative is presented as an alliance with either a liberal
or a police-state governmentality. That, it must be said, does
not constitute much of an alternative. Nevertheless, Foucault
at least sees socialism as a corrective to aspects of liberalism
– although he does not highlight the latter's problems. This
problematic remained with him during the early years of the
next decade – heightened, if anything, by the accusations
of a "silence of left-wing intellectuals" leveled by the socialist
government.[64] During these years, there was not only his
unfulfilled desire to write a book on the art of government
and socialist politics, possibly in the form of an interview
with Didier Eribon with the working title "La tête des socialistes."[65] There was also his close association with the Second
Left, associated with Michel Rocard's minor socialist party,
the PSU (Parti socialiste unifié [Unified Socialist Party]), and
particularly with a major trade union, the French Democratic
Confederation of Labor (Confederation française démocratique du travailleur, or CFDT). Their principal concern was
"self-management" (*autogestion*) understood as a decomposition and distribution of the state into a voluntary institution, and the freeing of the Socialist Party from "social
statism."[66] Foucault responded favorably to the work of the
major Second Left theorist Pierre Rosanvallon, and participated in the group's conferences.

Foucault goes as far as indicating Rosanvallon as the key
inspiration for, if not the source of, his view of liberalism, in

the Course Summary of *The Birth of Biopolitics.*[67] He calls
Rosanvallon's 1979 work *Le capitalisme utopique* an "important book," one that shows that "the market's role in the
liberal critique has been that of a 'test,' of a privileged site of
experiment in which one can pinpoint the effects of an excessive governmentality and take their measure."[68] Foucault
praises Rosanvallon's study as revealing that the aim of liberal
analysis was "to show the point at which governing was
always governing too much." Indeed, Foucault had already
turned Rosanvallon's conclusions into the founding principle
of liberalism: "one always governs too much."[69]

Foucault also contributed an interview entitled "A Finite
Social Security System Confronting an Infinite Demand" to
a collective work by the CFDT that was published in 1983
and has been available in English for many years.[70] Oddly
enough, it has been almost completely ignored by the governmentality literature, and rarely cited by Foucauldians[71] –
or others, for that matter. In this interview, conducted by the
then General Secretary of the union, Robert Bono, Foucault
diagnoses the current problems of social security as that
of "facing economic obstacles that are only too familiar,"
as being of limited use against the "political, economic
and social rationality of modern societies," and having the
"perverse effects" of "an increasing rigidity of certain mechanisms" and a "a growth of dependence."[72] This dependence
arises not from marginalization, as it historically had, but
from *integration* in the social security system itself.[73] His
answers to these problems are framed in terms of a "way of
life" and deploy the language of "lifestyles."[74] They seek a
"social security that opens the way to a richer, more numerous, more diverse, and more flexible relation with oneself and
one's environment," and that guarantees a "real autonomy."[75]
To combat welfare dependency, as many would later call it,
Foucault also suggests "a process of decentralization" that
would lead to a closer relation between users of services and
"decision-making centers."[76] In short, the structural economic problems of the fiscal crisis of the welfare state of his
time were to be met with new forms of subjectivation and
the decomposition of the state. In fact, he concludes that the
welfare system should become a "vast experimental field,"
and that the "whole institutional complex, at present very

fragile, will probably have to undergo a restructuring from top to bottom."[77] These few remarks, consonant with the orientation of the Second Left (and not altogether alien to what became Ewald's practice in the 1990s), give us a clue to what the book on the art of government and socialist politics might have looked like. They also have a certain familiarity for those of us who have taken more than a passing interest in the so-called "reform" of welfare states in the name of combating their self-produced dependency in recent decades.

It is true that Foucault never completed – or perhaps even really started – the proposed book, putting it aside to finalize the second and third volumes of *The History of Sexuality*. But, even allowing for the French intellectual idiom, it is supremely unlikely such a book would have ever functioned in the manner of Hayek's *The Road to Serfdom* or Milton Friedman's *Capitalism and Freedom* – that is, as a militant statement of a neoliberal philosophy intended for a large public. The closest example in the Anglophone world one can think of is perhaps that of Anthony Giddens's book *The Third Way*, published in 1998. Here a prominent thinker, social theorist and intellectual tried to cast a general policy framework – or a form of statecraft – for a newly elected center-Left government – in this case, the British Labour Party – that would learn from market-oriented philosophies and developments. Indeed, Colin Gordon has observed that "parts of the formulae of Clinton and Blair for a 'third way' may have effectively carried out a form of the operation which Foucault might have been taken as challenging the socialists to contemplate – the selective incorporation, in an updated and corrected social democracy, of certain elements of neoliberal analysis and strategy."[78] There is, however, at least one key difference between the English case and that of Foucault: where Giddens would deliberately move to elucidate a centrist position, Foucault continued to draw upon the radical practice of "self-management" (*autogestion*) advocated first by worker-militants in the takeover of workplaces such as the Lip factory he visited in July 1973.[79]

In this respect it should not surprise us that Foucault's understanding of neoliberalism has received favorable responses from both of the major schools he analyzed: the

Ordoliberals still residing in the Walter Eucken Institute in Freiburg[80] and the Chicago School. What makes Foucault's "apology" or "apologia" relevant, in retrospect, is not its distinctiveness but that it starts to mark out a now well-trodden intellectual pathway for progressive thought in the years following the postwar Long Boom and amidst trenchant questioning of Keynesian macro-economic policies and the welfare state from both Right and Left. He identifies a particular intellectual-political space, even if his ethos prevents him from fully occupying it.

Foucault beyond Foucault

So permit me now to move beyond these rather esoteric debates over Foucault's relationship to neoliberalism and indicate three inter-related themes that might allow us to move beyond Foucault but also, to the extent that they might contribute to a diagnostics of the present, to stay with him, or at least advance to the side of him.

The first of these themes is the problem of the market in Foucault, or rather the relationship between the market and truth. A fundamental thesis of *The Birth of Biopolitics* is that the market becomes the site of veridiction (or truth-telling) for liberalism and neoliberalism. This means quite simply that the "the market must tell the truth, it must tell the truth in relation to governmental practice."[81] A liberal art of government thus deploys the market as a regime of veridiction, so that it constitutes a "set of rules enabling one to establish which statements in a given discourse can be described as true or false."[82] There are, of course, different conceptions of the market: as natural or as constructed, as founded on exchange (Adam Smith), and as realizing the principle of competition (the Ordoliberals). But the idea of the market as a site for the production of truth and falsehood that is unknowable by the sovereign or its representatives brings us perilously close to Friedrich Hayek's view of the market as a kind of gigantic information processor, superior to highly limited human knowledge or the meddling of political actors. This leads to several problems for Foucault, concerning how to analyze the economy and how to approach neoliberalism. In his efforts to deconstruct the state, Foucault manages to produce another "cold monster," that of the market, and reproduces an asymmetry between the invisible hand of the market and the possibility of sovereign knowledge that is found in liberalism. Most important are the implications for state and public authority. While Foucault does indicate that "utility" acts as a measure internal to the assessment of public authority in classical liberalism, this measure is not a regime of veridiction but of "jurisdiction" – that is, of the legal delineation of public authority.[83] The de-centered and decomposed state, unlike the abstract and universal notion of the market, does not act as a principle of veridiction for governmental practice in Foucault. Hence, there is no analysis of how the idea of state "office" is governed by particular modes of truth-telling and comportment for the public servant – such as discretion, impartiality, and neutrality – which are supported by technologies of the self and styles of self-cultivation. One can refer to the work of Weberians such as Paul du Gay in this respect.[84] While Foucault views liberalism as fundamentally a critique of state reason, he fails to analyze the persistence of a state rationality within the liberal-democratic constitutional state and its forms of public authority.

There is no doubt that this can be remedied by Foucault's own work on forms of truth-telling or veridiction, particularly in his last two lecture series that deal with *parrhesia*,[85] and his schemata for the analysis of techniques of the self in the second and third volumes of *The History of Sexuality*.[86] These provide key resources for the task of analyzing the techniques of self-cultivation of the public official and the forms of truth-telling characteristic of public office. Such a project was indeed initiated by a group of thinkers originally located at Griffith University in Australia, in the mid-1990s.[87]

The second theme concerns the problem of inequality – or, rather, of inequality and subjectivity. By focusing on questions of subjugation and subjectivity, on the way in which we are subjectified in technologies of power and we work on ourselves in techniques of the self, Foucault belonged very much to the politics of his time – that is to say, the time of the post-revolutionary movements of the 1970s concerned with a politics of identity and difference: a "critical ontology of ourselves," as he would say. In our time – whatever weight we might give to the recent financial crisis and ongoing sovereign debt problems in Europe, or the movements against debt and the "one percent" in Europe and the United States, or indeed the notoriety of an economist such as Thomas Piketty – inequality has become again the target and focus of political action and debate. Foucault had very little to say about it. Perhaps his best word on it was the unsourced attribution to the Ordoliberal Wilhelm Röpke that "inequality is the same for all,"[88] which at least reminds us that the problematization of inequality in capitalist society does not necessarily augur greater equality.

The solutions Foucault offered for the crisis of the welfare state are very much to the point here. When defining the "present situation" in the interview on social security, Foucault rejected the idea of the structural social and economic situation, the "totality of economic and social mechanisms," and claimed to speak of the "relation between people's feelings, their moral choices, their relationship with themselves, and...the institutions that surround them."[89] In this respect, his solutions are not very different from those of a generation of social theorists and policy makers who would follow him, among them Giddens and Ulrich Beck. They would advocate active policies, life-planning, and reform in the name of individualization for clients of the welfare state, and new decentralized organizational forms. From the perspective of our time, after the nostrums of Labour's Third Way and US welfare reform under Clinton, and other such "experiments" from Australasia to the Nordic countries, the diagnosis and solutions that might have sounded somewhat fresh in Foucault's time are now rather depressingly familiar. We might say that the movements of the seventies (against institutionalization, over identity and the politics of difference) objected to the Marxist and socialist attempt to answer the question of subjectivity with that of inequality. What the history of welfare-state reform since the 1990s amply demonstrates is that it is not possible to answer questions of inequality in the language of subjectivity without intensifying domination and increasing inequality itself. We can use Foucauldian governmental and ethical analytics to analyze the demand for a work on the self in welfare rationalities and technologies. However, these frameworks must never be mistaken for social-theoretical recipes for how such practices *ought* to operate.

Finally, if Foucault creates a cold monster – in the economy – when he slays another – the state – this leaves him doubly disadvantaged with respect to an economic diagnosis of the present. First, he is disadvantaged with respect to the economy. Lazzarato has suggested that Foucault "neglects the functions of finance, debt and money."[90] This is because he is unable to think about economic relations per se and the mediation of relations of power through money and value.[91] In a very simple example, debt itself can be a form of the government of conduct: whether of the individuals who pledge much of their future to their creditors, or societies and states that have restricted public policy choices in the face of the aptly named sovereign debt. It might be that debt is the most effective way in which the contemporary neoliberal arts of government have managed to limit sovereignty and close down counter-conduct and contestation, and indeed the potential temporal horizons of our societies. In this sense, we might have to thank debt, not liberal democracy, for the End of History. Second, he is disadvantaged in that he is unable to move beyond the analysis of the rationalities and techniques of neoliberalism and the attempted production of the neoliberal subject to the analysis of the transformations of capital itself. While Foucault can examine how human capital theory – after Becker and his colleagues – enables a rationalization of public authority, and the enterprise acts as a paradigm for subjectivity, he fails to capture the intersection of capital and value with such rationalities and technologies. He fails to link "human capital" to the re-composition of capital, or to finance capital. In this respect, the interpretation and use of the Foucauldian legacy in the Italian autonomist tradition, associated with Negri and Lazzarato, with its emphasis on the way the post-disciplinary formation of subjectivity becomes fused to the co-creation of value, opens an avenue of further investigation.[92]

By a redistribution of the balance of risk and protection from the state and financial organizations to individuals, households, and welfare recipients, these rationalities and techniques have actively fostered increasing inequality. In redistributing debt, they increase general insecurity, destroy social bonds, and break down social cohesion – a theme on which Robert Castel[93] still has much to teach us. And in the absence of alternative narratives of social progress, we find a Europe reverting to atavistic nationalisms, anti-immigration policies, and worse. This, at the very least, constitutes one key vector of the history of our present, of our actuality, and of our contemporaneity. The conceptual tools of a fast-receding time are the legacy we have to begin with in this present, but they cannot, I submit, fully meet its demands.

Foucault is a notoriously difficult figure to pin down, particularly in respect of his political commitments, and he himself fiercely repudiated attempts to do so. We need to weigh his right not to be characterized against the urgent demands of our present. Even allowing for the former, I think it is fair to say that there is a consistency in his political alignments during the late 1970s and early 1980s toward elements on the French Left that were experimenting with neoliberal models of public policy. Like similar movements in Anglo-Saxon countries which would follow, these elements would imagine themselves as radical while occupying a kind of center of the political spectrum. At the same time, in opposition to the Socialist government, Pierre Bourdieu[94] would talk of a return to the tradition of a "libertarian Left" in opposition to the Left of the party machinery. Perhaps this term is as good as any to describe Foucault's general political orientation at this time.

Notes

1 Lecture delivered for "Remembering Foucault" event, Department of Law, London School of Economics, June 25, 2014. See M. Dean, "Michel Foucault's 'Apology' for Neoliberalism," *Journal of Political Power* 7, 3 (2014): 433–42, for the text as it was delivered that evening.

2 M. Foucault, *Naissance de la biopolitique. Cours au Collège de France, 1978–1979* (Paris: Gallimard, 2004).

3 J. Afary and K. B. Anderson, *Foucault and the Iranian Revolution: Gender and the Seductions of Islam* (Chicago, IL: University of Chicago Press, 2005), and A. Beaulieu, "Towards a Liberal

Utopia: The Connection between Foucault's Reporting on the Iranian Revolution and the Ethical Turn," *Philosophy and Social Criticism* 36, 7 (2010): 801–18.

4 M. Foucault, *The Birth of Biopolitics: Lectures at the Collège de France, 1978–1979*, trans. G. Burchell (London: Palgrave Macmillan, 2008), 188.

5 *Ibid.*, 78.

6 Ewald in G. Becker, F. Ewald, and B. Harcourt, *Becker on Ewald on Foucault on Becker: American Neoliberalism and Michel Foucault's 1979 "Birth of Biopolitics" Lectures*, Coase-Sandor Institute for Law and Economics Working Paper 614 (Chicago: University of Chicago Law School, 2012), 4.

7 Foucault, *The Birth of Biopolitics*, 188.

8 A. Negri, "Interview," *Le Monde*, October 3, 2001, available Libcom.org/library/interview-le-monde-negri.

9 M. Lazzarato, "Neoliberalism in Action: Inequality, Insecurity and the Reconstitution of the Social," *Theory, Culture and Society* 29, 6 (2009): 110.

10 J. Donzelot and C. Gordon, "Governing Liberal Societies: The Foucault Effect in the English-speaking World," *Foucault Studies 5* (January 2008): 55.

11 D. Macey, *The Lives of Michel Foucault* (London: Hutchinson, 1993), 301–5, and M. C. Behrent, "Accidents Happen: François Ewald, the 'Antirevolutionary Foucault,' and the Intellectual Politics of the French Welfare State," *Journal of Modern History* 82, 3 (2010): 585–624.

12 Behrent, "Accidents Happen," 619.

13 K. Villadsen and M. Dean, "State Phobia, Civil Society and a Certain Vitalism," *Constellations* 19, 3 (2012): 401–20.

14 Ewald, cited in Behrent, "Accidents Happen," 620–1.

15 Negri, "Interview."

16 C. Gordon, "Question, Ethos, Event," *Economy and Society* 15, 1 (1986): 74, and "Introduction," in G. Burchell, C. Gordon, and P. Miller, eds., *The Foucault Effect: Studies in Governmentality* (Hemel Hempstead: Harvester Wheatsheaf, 1991), 1–51, p. 7; and M. C. Behrent, "Liberalism without Humanism: Michel Foucault and the Free-market Creed, 1976–1979," chapter 2 in this volume.

17 Behrent, chapter 2 above, and "Accidents Happen."

18 T. Lemke, "The Birth of Bio-politics: Michel Foucault's Lecture at the Collège de France on Neo-liberal Governmentality," *Economy and Society* 30, 2 (2001): 190–207.

19 P. Dardot and C. Laval, *The New Way of the World: On Neoliberal Society*, trans. G. Elliot (London: Verso, 2013).

20 Foucault, *The Birth of Biopolitics*, 130.

21 Dardot and Laval, *The New Way of the World*, loc 178 (Kindle edition).

22 Lemke, "The Birth of Bio-Politics," 203.

23 *Ibid.*

24 Becker, Ewald, and Harcourt, *Becker on Ewald on Foucault on Becker*, 5.

25 *Ibid.*, 6.

26 *Ibid.*, 7.

27 Foucault, *The Birth of Biopolitics*, 269.

28 A. Dilts, "From 'Entrepreneur of the Self' to 'Care of the Self': Neo-liberal Governmentality and Foucault's Ethics," *Foucault Studies* 12 (2011): 133 n.11.

29 C. Gordon, "A Note on 'Becker on Ewald on Foucault on Becker. American Neoliberalism and Michel Foucault's 1979 "Birth of Biopolitics" lectures, a conversation with Gary Becker, François Ewald and Bernard Harcourt,'" *Foucault News* (February 2013): 1–14, available http://foucaultnews.files.wordpress.com/2013/02/colin-gordon-2013.pdf.

30 Becker, Ewald, and Harcourt, *Becker on Ewald on Foucault on Becker*, 3.

31 *Ibid.*, 17.

32 *Ibid.*, 18.

33 G. Becker, F. Ewald, and B. Harcourt, *Becker and Foucault on Crime and Punishment*, Coase-Sandor Institute for Law and Economics Working Paper 654 (Chicago: University of Chicago Law School, 2013), 2–3.

34 *Ibid.*, 9.

35 Foucault, *The Birth of Biopolitics*, 270.

36 Becker, Ewald, and Harcourt, *Becker and Foucault on Crime and Punishment*, 19.

37 P. Mirowski, *Never Let a Serious Crisis Go to Waste* (London: Verso, 2013), and P. Mirowski and D. Plehwe, eds., *The Road from Mont Pèlerin: The Making of the Neoliberal Thought Collective* (Cambridge, MA: Harvard University Press, 2009).

38 Becker, Ewald, and Harcourt, *Becker and Foucault on Crime and Punishment*, 21.

39 F. Ewald, "Foucault and the Contemporary Scene," *Philosophy and Social Criticism* 25, 3 (1999): 85.

40 *Ibid.*, 85.

41 *Ibid.*, 86–7.

42 *Ibid.*, 84, 90.

43 K. Tribe, "The Political Economy of Modernity: Foucault's Lectures at the Collège de France of 1978 and 1979," *Economy and Society* 38, 4 (2009): 685, and see M. Dean, *The Signature of*

Power: Sovereignty, Governmentality and Biopolitics (London: Sage, 2013), 71–6.

44 U. Tellmann, "Catastrophic Populations and the Fear of the Future: Malthus and the Genealogy of the Liberal Economy," *Theory, Culture and Society* 30, 2 (2013): 135–55, and Dean, *The Signature of Power*, 76–84, and "The Malthus Effect: Population and the Liberal Government of Life," *Economy and Society* 44, 1 (2015): 18–39.

45 M. Foucault, *Security, Territory, Population: Lectures at the Collège de France, 1977–1978*, trans. G. Burchell (London: Palgrave, 2007), 65.

46 Dean, *The Signature of Power*, 84–6.

47 G. Agamben, *The Kingdom and the Glory: For a Theological Genealogy of Economy and Government*, trans. L. Chiesa with M. Manderini (Stanford, CA: Stanford University Press, 2011), 110–11.

48 J. Spieker, "Defending the Open Society: Foucault, Hayek, and the Problem of Biopolitical Order," *Economy and Society* 42, 2 (2013): 304–21.

49 R. Ptak, "Neoliberalism in Germany: Revisiting the Ordoliberal Foundations of the Social Market Economy," in Mirowski and Plehwe, eds., *The Road from Mont Pèlerin*; and Dean, *The Signature of Power*, 178–83.

50 I. Hunter, "Uncivil Society: Liberal Government and the Deconfessionalisation of Politics," in M. Dean and B. Hindess, eds., *Governing Australia: Studies in Contemporary Rationalities of Government* (Cambridge: Cambridge University Press, 1998), 242–64.

51 D. Dupont and F. Pearce, "Foucault contra Foucault: Rereading the Governmentality Papers," *Theoretical Criminology* 5, 2 (2001): 123–58.

52 Hunter, "Uncivil Society."

53 Spieker, "Defending the Open Society of Biopolitical Order," 320.

54 P. Patton, "From Resistance to Government: Foucault's Lectures 1976–1979," in C. Falzon, T. O'Leary, and J. Sawicki, eds., *A Companion to Foucault* (Oxford: Blackwell, 2013), 186.

55 Foucault, *The Birth of Biopolitics*, 270.

56 *Ibid.*, 271.

57 Becker, Ewald, and Harcourt, *Becker on Ewald on Foucault on Becker*, 18.

58 Foucault, *The Birth of Biopolitics*, 259.

59 *Ibid.*, 259–60.

60 Beaulieu, "Towards a Liberal Utopia."

61 *Ibid.*, 812–13.

62 Foucault, *The Birth of Biopolitics*, 219.

63 *Ibid.*, 92–3.

64 D. Eribon, *Michel Foucault*, trans. B. Wing (Cambridge, MA: Harvard University Press, 1991), 296–306.

65 Foucault, *The Birth of Biopolitics*, 100 n.53, and Eribon, *Michel Foucault*, 306–7.

66 Behrent, "Liberalism without humanism," chapter 2 in this volume.

67 Foucault, *The Birth of Biopolitics*, 320.

68 *Ibid.*

69 *Ibid*, 319.

70 Foucault, "Social Security," in Foucault, *Politics, Philosophy, Culture: Interviews and Other Writings 1977–84*, ed. L. D. Kritzman (New York: Routledge, 1988), 159–77.

71 But see C. Gordon, "Foucault in Britain," in *Foucault and Political Reason: Liberalism, Neo-liberalism and Rationalities of Government*, ed. A. Barry, T. Osborne, and N. Rose (London: UCL Press, 1996), 253–70.

72 Foucault, "Social Security," 160.

73 *Ibid.*, 162.

74 *Ibid.*, 164–5.

75 *Ibid.*, 161.

76 *Ibid.*, 165.

77 *Ibid.*, 166.

78 Donzelot and Gordon, "Governing Liberal Societies," 52.

79 D. Defert, "Chronology," in Falzon, O'Leary, and Sawicki, eds., *A Companion to Foucault*, 54.

80 N. Goldschmidt and H. Rauchenschwandtner, *The Philosophy of Social Market Economy: Michel Foucault's Analysis of Ordoliberalism*. Freiburg Discussion Papers on Constitutional Economics 07/4 (Freiburg: Walter Eucken Institute, 2007).

81 Foucault, *The Birth of Biopolitics*, 32.

82 *Ibid.*, 35.

83 *Ibid.*, 44.

84 P. Du Gay, *In Praise of Bureaucracy: Weber, Organization, Ethics* (London: Sage, 2000).

85 M. Foucault, *The Government of Self and Others: Lectures at the Collège de France, 1982–1983*, trans. G. Burchell (London: Palgrave, 2010), and *The Courage of Truth: The Government of Self and Others II: Lectures at the Collège de France, 1983–1984*, trans. G. Burchell (London: Palgrave, 2011).

86 M. Foucault, *The History of Sexuality*, vol. II, *The Use of Pleasure*, trans. R. Hurley (New York: Pantheon, 1985), and *The*

History of Sexuality, vol. III, *The Care of the Self*, trans. R. Hurley (New York: Pantheon, 1986).

87 I. Hunter, "Personality as a Vocation," *Economy and Society* 19, 4 (1990): 391–430, and J. Minson, "Ethics in the Service of the State," in Dean and Hindess, eds., *Governing Australia*, 47–69.

88 Foucault, *The Birth of Biopolitics*, 143.

89 Foucault, "Social Security," 161–2.

90 M. Lazzarato, *The Making of Indebted Man: An Essay on the Neoliberal Condition*, trans. J. D. Jordan (Los Angeles, CA: Semiotext(e), 2012), 90.

91 U. Tellmann, "Foucault and the Invisible Economy," *Foucault Studies* 6 (2009): 8.

92 T. Lopdrup-Hjorth, *Let's Go Outside: The Value of Co-creation*. Doctoral School of Organization and Management Studies, Copenhagen Business School (2013).

93 R. Castel, *From Manual Workers to Wage Laborers: Transformation of the Social Question*, trans. Richard Boyd (New Brunswick, NJ: Transaction, 2003).

94 Eribon, *Michel Foucault*, 301.

5

Bourdieu, Foucault, and the Penal State in the Neoliberal Era

Loïc Wacquant

Three analytic breaks proved indispensable to diagnosing the invention of a new government of social insecurity wedding supervisory "workfare" and castigatory "prisonfare," dissected in my book *Punishing the Poor*, and to accounting for the punitive policy turn taken by the United States and other advanced societies following its lead onto the path of economic deregulation and welfare retrenchment in the closing decades of the twentieth century.[1]

The first consists in escaping the crime-and-punishment poke, which continues to straitjacket scholarly and policy debates on incarceration, even as the divorce of this familiar couple grows ever more barefaced.[2] The second break requires relinking social welfare and penal policies, inasmuch as these two strands of government action toward the poor have come to be informed by the same behaviorist philosophy relying on deterrence, surveillance, stigma, and graduated sanctions to modify conduct. Welfare revamped as workfare and the prison stripped of its rehabilitative pretension now form a single organizational mesh flung at the same clientele mired in the fissures and ditches of the dualizing metropolis – namely, the urban precariat, chief among them the dispossessed and dishonored residents of the hyperghetto. The third rupture involves overcoming the conventional opposition between materialist and symbolic approaches, descended from the emblematic figures of Karl Marx and Émile Durkheim respectively, so as to heed and hold together the instrumental and the expressive functions of the penal apparatus. Weaving together concerns for control and communication, the management of derelict categories and the affirmation of salient social borders makes it possible to go beyond an analysis couched in the language of prohibition to trace how the rolling out of the prison and its institutional tentacles (probation, parole, criminal databases, swirling discourses about crime, and a virulent culture of public denigration of offenders) has reshaped the sociosymbolic landscape and remade the state itself.

A single self-same concept sufficed to effect those three breaks simultaneously and to sketch the anatomy of the penal state in the era of triumphant neoliberalism: the notion of *bureaucratic field* developed by Pierre Bourdieu, in his lecture course at the Collège de France in the early 1990s,[3] to rethink the state as the agency that monopolizes the legitimate use not only of material violence (as in Max Weber's well-known capsule), but also of symbolic violence, and that moulds social space and strategies by setting the conversion rate between the various species of capital. It is useful to briefly confront and contrast my derivation of Bourdieu's theory of the state with the classic theses of Michel Foucault on punishment in *Surveiller et punir* (in English, *Discipline and Punish*).[4] This will allow me to clarify the analytic implications of my model of the punitive turn in the management of precarized populations in advanced society, but also to open a dialogue between Bourdieu and Foucault on the carceral front. This dialogue helps us better locate penality in the forging of state and citizenship in the twenty-first century and brooks further elaboration.

Bourdieu and the bolstering of the Right hand of the state

In *The Weight of the World* and related essays, Pierre Bourdieu proposes that we construe the state not as a monolithic and coordinated ensemble, but as a splintered space of forces vying over the definition and distribution of public goods which he calls the "bureaucratic field."[5] The constitution of this space is the end-result of a long-term process of concentration of the various species of capital operative in a given social formation, and especially of "juridical capital as the objectified and codified form of symbolic capital" which enables the state to monopolize the official definition of identities, the promulgation of standards of conduct, and the administration of justice.[6]

In the contemporary period, the bureaucratic field is traversed by two internecine struggles. The first pits the "higher state nobility" of policy makers intent on promoting market-oriented reforms against the "lower state nobility" of executants attached to the traditional missions of government inherited from the Fordist–Keynesian period. The second opposes what Bourdieu, riffing off Hobbes's classic portrayal of the ruler, calls the "Left hand" and the "Right hand" of the state. The Left hand, the feminine side of Leviathan, is materialized by the "spendthrift" ministries in charge of "social functions" – public education, health, housing, social welfare, and labor law – which offer protection and succor to the social categories shorn of economic and cultural capital. The Right hand, the masculine side, is charged with enforcing the new economic discipline via budget cuts, fiscal incentives, and economic "deregulation" (i.e. re-regulation in favor of firms).

By inviting us to grasp in a single conceptual framework the various sectors of the state that administer the life conditions and chances of the working class and assorted problem populations, and to view these sectors as enmeshed in relations of antagonistic cooperation as they vie for preeminence inside the bureaucratic field, this conception has helped us map the ongoing shift from the social to the penal treatment of urban marginality. In this regard, *Punishing the Poor* fills in a gap in Bourdieu's model by inserting the police, the courts, and *the prison as core constituents of the "Right hand"* of the state, alongside the ministries of the economy and the budget. It suggests that we need to bring penal policies from the periphery to the center of our analysis of the redesign and deployment of government programs aimed at coping with the entrenched poverty and deepening disparities spawned in the polarizing city by the discarding of the Fordist–Keynesian social compact.[7]

The new government of social insecurity put in place in the United States and offered as model to other advanced countries entails both a shift from the social to the penal wing of the state (detectible in the reallocation of public budgets, personnel, and discursive precedence) and the colonization of the welfare sector by the panoptic and punitive logic characteristic of the post-rehabilitation penal bureaucracy (as with programs that mandate the drug-testing of welfare applicants). The slanting of state activity from the social to the penal arm and the incipient penalization of welfare, in turn, partake of the *remasculinization of the state*, in reaction to the wide-ranging changes provoked in the political field by the women's movement and by the institutionalization of social rights antinomic to commodification. The new priority given to duties over rights, sanction over support, the stern rhetoric of the "obligations of citizenship," and the martial reaffirmation of the capacity of the state to lock the troublemaking poor (welfare recipients and criminals) "in a subordinate relation of dependence and obedience" toward state managers portrayed as virile protectors of the society against its wayward members:[8] all these policy planks pronounce and promote the transition from the kindly "nanny state" of the Fordist–Keynesian era to the strict "daddy state" of neoliberalism.

In their classic study *Regulating the Poor*, Frances Fox Piven and Richard Cloward forged a germinal model of the management of poverty in industrial capitalism. According to this model, the state expands or contracts its relief programs cyclically to respond to the ups and downs of the economy, the corresponding slackening and tightening of the labor market, and the bouts of social disruption that increased unemployment and destitution trigger periodically among the lower class. Phases of welfare expansion serve to "mute civil disorders" that threaten established hierarchies, while phases of restriction aim to "enforce work norms" by pushing recipients back onto the labor market.[9] *Punishing the Poor* contends that, while this model worked well for the age of Fordist industrialism and accounts for the two major welfare explosions witnessed in the United States during the Great Depression and the affluent but turbulent 1960s, it has been rendered obsolete by the neoliberal remaking of the state over the past quarter-century. In the age of fragmented labor, hypermobile capital, and sharpening social inequalities and anxieties, the "central role of relief in the regulation of marginal labor and in the maintenance of social order"[10] is displaced and duly supplemented by the vigorous deployment of the police, the courts, and the prison in the nether regions of social space. To the single oversight of the poor by the Left hand of the state succeeds the *double regulation of poverty by the joint action of punitive welfare-turned-workfare and an agressive penal bureaucracy*. The cyclical alternation of contraction and expansion of public aid is replaced by the continual contraction of welfare and the runaway expansion of prisonfare.[11]

This organizational coupling of the left hand and right hand of the state under the aegis of the same disciplinary philosophy of behaviorism and moralism can be understood, first, by recalling the shared historical origins of poor relief and penal confinement in the chaotic passage from feudalism to capitalism. Both policies were devised in the long sixteenth century to "absorb and regulate the masses of discontented people uprooted" by this epochal transition.[12] Similarly, both policies were overhauled in the last two decades of the twentieth century in response to the socioeconomic dislocations provoked by neoliberalism: in the 1980s alone, in addition to reducing public assistance, California passed nearly 1,000 laws expanding the use of prison sentences; at the federal level, the 1996 reform that "ended welfare as we know it" was complemented by the sweeping Violent Crime Control and Law Enforcement Act of 1993 (which stipulates the single largest increase in penal sanctions in US history) and bolstered by the No Frills Prison Act of 1995 (which funds the expansion of the prison system and eliminates incentives to rehabilitation).

The institutional pairing of public aid and incarceration as tools for managing the unruly poor can also be understood by paying attention to the structural, functional, and cultural similarities between workfare and prisonfare as "people processing institutions" targeted on kindred problem populations.[13] It has been facilitated by the transformation of welfare in a punitive direction and the activation of the penal system to handle more of the traditional clientele of assistance to the destitute – the incipient "penalization" of welfare matching the degraded "welfarization" of the prison. Their concurrent reform over the past 30 years has helped cement their organizational convergence, even as they have obeyed inverse principles. The gradual erosion of public aid and its revamping into workfare in 1996 has entailed restricting entry into the system, shortening "stays" on the rolls, and speeding up exit, resulting in a spectacular reduction of the stock of beneficiaries (it plummeted from nearly 5 million households in 1992 to under 2 million a decade later). Trends in penal policy have followed the exact opposite tack: admission into jail and prison has been greatly facilitated, sojourns behind bars lengthened, and releases curtailed, which has yielded a spectacular ballooning of the population under lock and key (it jumped by over 1 million in the 1990s). The operant purpose of welfare shifted from passive "people-processing" to active "people-changing" after 1988, and especially after the abolition of AFDC (Aid to Families with Dependent Children, the main poor relief program) in 1996, while the prison has traveled in the other direction, from aiming to reform inmates (under the philosophy of rehabilitation, hegemonic from the 1920s to the mid-1970s) to merely warehousing them (as the function of punishment was downgraded to retribution and neutralization).

The shared historical roots, organizational isomorphism, and operational convergence of the assistential and penitential poles of the bureaucratic field in the United States are further fortified by the fact that the social profiles of their beneficiaries are virtually identical. Recipients of AFDC (the main targeted welfare program until 1996) and jail inmates both live near, or below, 50% of the federal poverty line (for one-half and two-thirds of them, respectively); both are disproportionately black and hispanic (37% and 18% for inmates versus 41% and 19% for welfare recipients); the majority did not finish high school and are saddled with serious physical and mental disabilities interfering with their participation in the workforce (44% of AFDC mothers as against 37% of jail inmates). And they are closely bound to one another by extensive kin, marital, and social ties, reside overwhelmingly in the same impoverished households and barren neighborhoods, and face the same bleak life horizon at the bottom of the class and ethnic structure.

Punishing the Poor avers not only that the United States has shifted from the single (welfare) to the double (social-*cum*-penal) regulation of the poor, but also that "the stunted development of American social policy" skillfully dissected by Piven and Cloward[14] stands in close causal and functional relation to America's uniquely overgrown and hyperactive penal policy. *The misery of American welfare and the grandeur of American prisonfare at century's turn are the two sides of the same political coin.* The generosity of the latter is in direct proportion to the stinginess of the former, and it expands to the degree that both are driven by moral behaviorism. The same structural features of the American state – its bureaucratic fragmentation and ethnoracial skew, the institutional bifurcation between universalist "social insurance" and categorical "welfare," and the market-buttressing cast of assistance programs – that facilitated the organized atrophy of welfare in reaction to the racial crisis of the 1960s and the economic turmoil of the 1970s have also fostered the uncontrolled hypertrophy of punishment aimed at the same precarious population. Moreover, the "tortured impact of slavery and institutionalized racism on the construction of the American polity" has been felt not only in the "underdevelopment" of public aid, and the "decentralized and fragmented government and party system" that distributes it to a select segment of the dispossessed,[15] but also in the overdevelopment and stupendous severity of its penal wing. Ethnoracial division and the (re)activation of the stigma of blackness as dangerousness are key to explaining the initial atrophy and accelerating decay of the American social state in the post-Civil Rights epoch, on the one hand, and the astonishing ease and celerity with which the penal state arose on its ruins, on the other.[16]

Reversing the historical bifurcation of the labor and crime questions achieved in the late nineteenth century, *punitive containment* as a government technique for managing deepening urban marginality has effectively rejoined social and penal policy at the close of the twentieth century. It taps the diffuse social anxiety coursing through the middle and lower regions of social space in reaction to the splintering of wage work and the resurgence of inequality, and converts it into popular animus toward welfare recipients and street criminals, cast as twin detached and defamed categories which sap the social order by their dissolute morality and dissipated behavior and must therefore be placed under severe tutelage. The new government of poverty invented by the United States to enforce the normalization of social insecurity thus gives a whole new meaning to the notion of "poor relief": punitive containment offers relief not *to* the poor but *from* the poor, by forcibly "disappearing" the most disruptive of them, from the shrinking welfare rolls on the one hand and into the swelling dungeons of the carceral castle on the other.

Foucault and the perfusion of "the carceral"

Michel Foucault has put forth the single most influential analysis of the rise and role of the prison in capitalist modernity, and it is useful to set my thesis against the rich tapestry of analyses he has stretched and stimulated.[17] I concur with the author of *Discipline and Punish* that penality is a protean force that is eminently fertile and must be given pride of place in the study of contemporary power.[18] While its originary medium resides in the application of legal coercion to enforce the core strictures of the sociomoral order, punishment must be viewed not through the narrow and technical prism of repression but by recourse to the notion of production. The assertive rolling out of the penal state has indeed engendered new categories and discourses, novel administrative bodies and government policies, fresh social types and associated forms of knowledge across the criminal and social welfare domains.[19] But, from here, my argument diverges sharply from Foucault's view of the emergence and functioning of the punitive society in at least four ways.

To start with, Foucault erred in spotting the retreat of the penitentiary. Disciplines may have diversified and metastasized to thrust sinewy webs of control across the society, but the prison has not for all that receded from the historical stage and "lost its raison d'être."[20] On the contrary, penal confinement has made a stunning comeback and reaffirmed itself among the central missions of Leviathan, just as Foucault and his followers were forecasting its demise: there were fewer than 25,000 inmates in France in 1975; they now number close to 70,000. And carceral expansion is a deep and broad trend sweeping both the First and Second worlds: in the quarter-century following the publication of *Discipline and Punish*, the incarceration rate doubled in France, Italy, and Belgium; it nearly tripled in England, Sweden, and the Netherlands; and it quadrupled in the United States. It also grew spectacularly across Latin America as the continent made the "double transition" to electoral democracy and the global market, and it boomed across Eastern Europe in the wake of the collapse of the Soviet empire. After the founding burst of the 1600s and the consolidation of the 1800s, the turn of the present century ranks as the third "age of confinement" that penologist Thomas Mathiesen[21] forewarned about in 1990.

Next, whatever their uses in the eighteenth century, disciplinary technologies have *not* been deployed inside the overgrown and voracious carceral system of our *fin de siècle*. Hierarchical classification, elaborate time schedules, non-idleness, close-up examination, and the regimentation of the body: these techniques of penal "normalization" have been rendered wholly impracticable by the demographic chaos spawned by overpopulation, bureaucratic rigidity, resource depletion, and the studious indifference – if not hostility – of penal authorities toward rehabilitation.[22] In lieu of the *dressage* ("training" or "taming") intended to fashion "docile and productive bodies" postulated by Foucault, the contemporary prison is geared toward brute neutralization, rote retribution, and simple warehousing – by default, if not by design. If there are "engineers of consciousness" and "orthopedists of individuality" at work in the mesh of disciplinary powers today,[23] they surely are not employed by departments of corrections.

In the third place, "devices for normalization" anchored in the carceral institution have *not* spread throughout the society, in the manner of capillaries irrigating the entire body social. Rather, the widening of the penal dragnet under neoliberalism has been remarkably discriminating: in spite of conspicuous bursts of corporate crime (epitomized by the Savings and Loans scandal of the late 1980s, the folding of Enron a decade later, and the "subprime" crash of 2008) with devastating economic and human consequences, it has affected essentially the denizens of the lower regions of social and physical space. Indeed, the fact that the social and ethnoracial selectivity of the prison has been maintained – nay, reinforced – as it vastly enlarged its intake demonstrates that penalization is not an all-encompassing master logic that blindly traverses the social order to bend and bind its various constituents. On the contrary: it is a *skewed technique proceeding along sharp gradients of class, ethnicity, and place,*[24] and it operates to divide populations and to differentiate categories according to established conceptions of moral worth. At the dawn of the twenty-first century, America's urban (sub)proletariat lives in a "punitive society," but its middle and upper classes certainly do not. Similarly, efforts to import and adapt US-style slogans and methods of law-enforcement – such as zero tolerance policing, mandatory minimum sentencing, or boot camps for juveniles – in Europe have been trained on lower-class and immigrant offenders relegated to the defamed neighborhoods at the center of the panic over "ghettoization" that has swept across the continent during the past decade.[25]

Lastly, the crystallization of *law-and-order pornography*, that is, the accelerating inflection and inflation of penal activity conceived, represented, and implemented for the primary purpose of being displayed in ritualized form by the authorities – the paradigm for which is the half-aborted reintroduction of chain gangs in striped uniforms in several Southern states – suggests that news of the death of the "spectacle of the scaffold" has been greatly exaggerated. The "redistribution" of "the whole economy of punishment"[26] in the post-Fordist period has entailed not its disappearance from public view, as proposed by Foucault, but its institutional relocation, symbolic elaboration, and social proliferation beyond anything anyone envisioned when *Discipline and Punish* was published.

In the past quarter-century, a whole galaxy of novel cultural and social forms – indeed, a veritable industry trading on representations of offenders and law-enforcement – has sprung forth and spread. The theatralization of penality has migrated from the state to the commercial media and the political field *in toto*, and it has extended from the final ceremony of sanction to encompass the full penal chain, with a privileged place accorded to police operations in low-income districts and courtroom confrontations around celebrity defendants. The Place de grève, where the regicide Damiens was famously quartered, has thus been supplanted not by the panopticon but by *Court TV* and the profusion of crime-and-punishment "reality shows" that have inundated television (*Cops, 911, America's Most Wanted, American Detective, Bounty Hunters, Inside Cell Block F*, etc.), not to mention the use of criminal justice as fodder for the daily news and dramatic series (*Law and Order, CSI, Prison Break, Orange is the New Black*, etc.). This is to say that the prison did not "replace" the "social game of the signs of punishment and the garrulous feast that put them in motion."[27] Rather, it now serves as its institutional canopy. Everywhere the law-and-order *guignol* has become a core civic theater onto whose stage elected officials prance to dramatize moral norms and display their professed capacity for decisive action, thereby reaffirming the political relevance of Leviathan at the very moment when they organize its powerlessness with respect to the market.

In short, lacking a structural concept with which to anchor penality as a form of symbolic power accumulating in the higher reaches of social space (what Bourdieu captures with the notion of "field of power"), Foucault misread the historical trend of modern Western penality when he prophesied the vanishing of the prison at the very moment it was entering a phase of rapid expansion and wholesale solidification. He consistently conflated the blueprints of penal reformers and the prescriptions of theorists of confinement with the everyday reality of imprisonment, ignoring the fact that the social organization of the carceral institution[28] renders it constitutively incapable of "making the accumulation of men docile and useful."[29] Accordingly, he mischaracterized the tenor of "the carceral," exaggerated its diffusion, and overlooked both the steep selectivity of penalization and the enduring centrality of punishment to the symbolic projection and material exercise of state power.[30]

The neoliberal state and the double regulation of poverty

The invention of the double regulation of the insecure fractions of the postindustrial proletariat via the wedding of social and penal policy at the bottom of the polarized class structure is a major *structural innovation* that takes us beyond the model of the welfare–poverty nexus elaborated by Piven and Cloward[31] just as the Fordist–Keynesian regime was coming unglued. The birth of this institutional contraption is also not captured by Michel Foucault's vision of the "disciplinary society" or by David Garland's[32] notion of the "culture of control," neither of which can account for the unforeseen timing, steep socioethnic selectivity, and peculiar organizational path of the abrupt turnaround in penal trends in the closing decades of the twentieth century. For the punitive containment of urban marginality through the simultaneous rolling back of the social safety net and the rolling out of the police-and-prison dragnet, and their knitting together into a carceral–assistential lattice, is not the spawn of some broad societal trend – whether it be the ascent of "biopower" or the advent of "late modernity" – but, at bottom, an exercise in *state crafting*. It partakes of the correlative revamping of the perimeter, missions, and capacities of public authority on the economic, social welfare, and penal fronts. This revamping has been uniquely swift, broad, and deep in the United States, but it is in progress – or in question – in all advanced societies subject to the relentless material and ideological pressure to conform to the American pattern.

Consider trends in France: in recent years, the country has eased strictures on part-time employment, as well as limitations on night-time and week-end work. Its governments of both the Left and the Right have actively supported the development of short-term contracts, temporary jobs, and underpaid traineeships, and expanded the latitude of employers in hiring, firing, and the use of overtime. The result is that the number of precarious wage earners has risen from 1.7 million in 1992 to 2.8 million in 2007 – or from 8.6 to 12.4% of the employed workforce.[33] In June of 2009, France instituted the RSA (Revenu de solidarité active), set to gradually replace the RMI (Revenu minimum d'insertion, the guaranteed minimum income grant provided to some 1.3 million), a program designed to push public aid recipients into the low-wage labor market via state subsidies to poor workers premised on the obligation to accept employment.[34] Simultaneously, the oversight of unemployment benefits is being farmed out to private firms, which can terminate beneficiaries who reject two job offers, and receive a financial bonus for each recipient they place in a job. On the penal front, accelerating the punitive turn taken by the Socialist government of Jospin in 1998–2002, the successive administrations of Chirac and Sarkozy have adopted sweeping measures of penal expansion:[35] intensified policing centered on low-income districts, youth night curfews, enlarged recourse to incarceration for street crimes (in sharp contrast to the depenalization of corporate crime), plea bargaining and accelerated judicial processing for low-level delinquents, mandatory minimum sentences for youth recidivists, annual targets for the expulsion of undocumented migrants, and the indefinite civil commitment of certain categories of sex offenders after they have served their sentence. The country's budget for corrections jumped from 1.4 billion euros for 22,000 guards confining 48,000 inmates in 2001, to 3.1 billion euros for 37,000 guards and 67,000 inmates in 2013 – a far cry from the vanishing of the prison prophesied by Foucault three decades earlier.

Tracking the roots and modalities of America's stupendous drive to hyperincarceration opens a unique path into the *sanctum* of the neoliberal Leviathan. It leads us to articulate two major theoretical claims. The first is that *the penal apparatus is a core organ of the state*, expressive of its sovereignty and instrumental in imposing categories, upholding material and symbolic divisions, and molding relations and behaviors through the selective penetration of social and physical space. The police, the courts, and the prison are not mere technical appendages for the enforcement of lawful order (as criminology would have it), but vehicles for the political production of reality and for the oversight of deprived and defamed social categories and their reserved territories.[36] Students of early modern state formation, from Norbert Elias to Charles Tilly to Gianfranco Poggi, fully recognized that the monopolization of force, and thus the construction of a bureaucratic machinery for policing, judging, and punishing miscreants capable of minimally pacifying society, was central to the building of Leviathan. It is high time that students of the neoliberal era noticed that the remaking of the state after the break-up of the Keynesian social compact has entailed not only renewed activity aimed at fostering international competitiveness, technological innovation, and labor flexibility,[37] but also – and most distinctively – the forceful reassertion of its penal mission, henceforth set in a pornographic and managerialist key.

Indeed, the second thesis advanced by *Punishing the Poor* is that the ongoing capitalist "revolution from above," commonly called *neoliberalism, entails the enlargement and exaltation of the penal sector* of the bureaucratic field, so that the state may check the social reverberations caused by the diffusion of social insecurity in the lower rungs of the class and ethnic hierarchy, as well as assuage popular discontent over the dereliction of its traditional economic and social duties. Neoliberalism readily resolves what for Garland's "culture of control" remains an enigmatic paradox of late modernity: namely, the fact that "control is now being re-emphasized in every area of social life – *with the singular and startling exception of the economy*, from whose deregulated domain most of today's major risks routinely emerge."[38] The neoliberal remaking of the state also explains the steep class, ethnoracial, and spatial bias stamping the simultaneous retraction of its social bosom and expansion of its penal fist: the populations most directly and adversely impacted by the convergent revamping of the labor market and public aid turn out also to be the privileged "beneficiaries" of the penal largesse of the authorities. This is true in the United States, where the carceral boom has corralled (sub)proletarian blacks trapped in the bare hyperghetto. It is also the case in Western Europe, where the primary clientele of the expanding prison is composed of precarious workers and the unemployed, postcolonial migrants, and lower-class addicts and derelicts.[39]

Finally, neoliberalism correlates closely with the international diffusion of punitive policies in both the welfare and the criminal domains. It is not by accident that the advanced countries that have imported, first, workfare measures designed to buttress the discipline of desocialized wage work, and then variants of US-style criminal justice measures, are the Commonwealth nations that also pursued aggressive policies of economic deregulation inspired by the "free market" nostrums come from America, whereas the countries that remained committed to a strong regulatory state curbing social insecurity have best resisted the sirens of "zero tolerance" policing and "prison works."[40] Similarly, societies of the Second World such as Brazil, Argentina, and South Africa, which adopted superpunitive penal planks inspired by American developments in the 1990s and saw their prison populations soar as a result, did so not because they had at long last reached the stage of "late modernity," but because they have taken the route of market deregulation and social retrenchment.[41] But to discern these multilevel connections between the upsurge of the punitive Leviathan and the spread of neoliberalism, it is necessary to develop a precise and broad conception of the latter. Instead of discarding neoliberalism, as Garland does, on account of it being "rather too specific" a phenomenon to account for penal escalation,[42] we must expand our conception of it, and move from an economic to a fully sociological understanding of the phenomenon.

By enabling us to break out of the crime-and-punishment box to relink welfare and justice while fully attending to both the material and symbolic dimensions of public policy, Bourdieu's concept of bureaucratic field opens a way out of the cul-de-sac into which Foucault directed us, and offers a powerful tool for dissecting the anatomy and assembly of the neoliberal Leviathan. It suggests that some of the pivotal political struggles of this century's turn – if not the most visible or salient ones – involve not the confrontation between the mobilized organizations representing subaltern categories and the state, but battles internal to the hierarchical and dynamic ensemble of public bureaucracies that compete to socialize, medicalize, or penalize urban marginality and its correlates. Elucidating the nexus of workfare, prisonfare, and social insecurity, in turn, reveals that the study of incarceration is neither a technical rubric in the criminological catalogue nor a dying subspecies of proliferating disciplines but a key chapter in the sociology of the state and social inequality in the bloom of neoliberalism.

Notes

1 This chapter is extracted and adapted from the "theoretical coda" of my book *Punishing the Poor: The Neoliberal Government of Social Insecurity* (Durham, NC, and London: Duke University Press, 2009). The overarching argument of the book unfolds in four steps. Part 1 maps out the accelerating decline and abiding misery of America's social state, climaxing with the replacement of protective welfare by disciplinary workfare in 1996. Part 2 tracks the modalities of the growth and grandeur of the penal state and finds that the coming of "carceral big government" was driven not by trends in criminality, but by the class and racial backlash against the social advances of the 1960s. Part 3 heeds the communicative dimension of penality as a vehicle for symbolic boundary-drawing and explains why penal activism in the United States has been aimed at two "privileged targets," the black subproletariat trapped in the imploding ghetto and the roaming sex offender. Part 4 follows recent declinations of the new politics of social insecurity in Western Europe to offer a critique of the "scholarly myths" of the reigning law-and-order reason, prescriptions for escaping the punitive policy snare, and a characterization of the distinctive shape and missions of the neoliberal state.

2 A simple statistic suffices to demonstrate this disconnect and reveals the futility of trying to explain rising incarceration by escalating crime: the United States held 21 prisoners for every 1,000 "index crimes" in 1975, compared to 113 convicts per 1,000 crimes in 2000, for an increase of 438 percent; for "violent crimes," the jump is from 231 to 922 convicts per 1,000 offenses, an increase of 299 percent. This means that the country became four to five times more punitive in a quarter-century *holding crime constant* (a lagged index turns up the same trend). For elaborations, see Wacquant, *Punishing the Poor*, 125–33.

3 P. Bourdieu, "Rethinking the State: On the Genesis and Structure of the Bureaucratic Field," *Sociological Theory* 12, 1 (1994 [1993]): 1–19.

4 M. Foucault, *Surveiller et punir. Naissance de la prison* (Paris: Gallimard, 1975); *Discipline and Punish: The Birth of the Prison* (New York: Vintage, 1977).

5 The concept is sketched analytically in Bourdieu, "Rethinking the State"; illustrated in Bourdieu, "The Abdication of the State," in Bourdieu et al., eds., *The Weight of the World: Social Suffering in Contemporary Society* (Cambridge: Polity, 1999), 181–8; and deployed to probe the political production of the economy of single homes in France in Bourdieu, *The Social Structures of the Economy*

(Cambridge: Polity, 2005 [2000]). The historical emergence and analytic construction of the bureaucratic field is sketched in Bourdieu's lecture course *On The State* (Cambridge: Polity, 2015). Several issues of the journal *Actes de la recherche en sciences sociales* offer further crossnational empirical illustrations, including those on "The History of the State" (nos. 116–17, March 1997), "The Genesis of the State" (no. 118, June 1997), the transition "From Social State to Penal State" (no. 124, September 1998), "Pacify and Punish" (nos. 173 and 174, June and September 2008), and "Reasons of State" (nos. 201 and 202, March 2014).

6 Bourdieu, "Rethinking the State," 4, 9.

7 S. Musterd, A. Murie, and C. Kesteloot, *Neighbourhoods of Poverty: Urban Social Exclusion and Integration in Comparison* (London: Palgrave Macmillan, 2006); W. J. Wilson, *When Work Disappears: The World of the New Urban Poor* (New York: Knopf, 1996); and L. Wacquant, *Urban Outcasts: A Comparative Sociology of Advanced Marginality* (Cambridge: Polity, 2008).

8 I. M. Young, "The Logic of Masculinist Protection: Reflections on the Current Security State," in M. Friedman, ed., *Women and Citizenship* (New York: Oxford University Press, 2005), 15–34.

9 F. Fox Piven and R. A. Cloward, *Regulating the Poor: The Functions of Public Welfare* (New York: Vintage, 1993 [1971]): xvi and passim.

10 *Ibid.*, xviii.

11 By analogy with "welfare," I designate by "prisonfare" the policy stream through which the state gives a penal response to festering urban ills and sociomoral disorders, as well as the imagery, discourses, and bodies of lay and expert knowledge that accrete around the rolling out of the police, the courts, jails and prisons, and their extensions (probation, parole, computerized data-banks of criminal files, and the schemes of remote profiling and surveillance they enable). Penalization joins socialization and medicalization as the three alternative strategies whereby the state can opt to treat undesirable conditions and conducts (Wacquant, *Punishing the Poor*, 16–17).

12 Fox Piven and Cloward, *Regulating the Poor*, 21, and 20 n.23, acknowledge penal expansion and activism in the sixteenth century in passing in the rich historical recapitulation of the trajectory of poor relief in early modern Europe in which they ground their investigation of the functions of welfare in contemporary America.

13 Y. Hasenfeld, "People Processing Organizations: An Exchange Approach," *American Sociological Review* 37, 3 (1972): 256–63.

14 Fox Piven and Cloward, *Regulating the Poor*, 409.

15 *Ibid.*, 424–5.

16 The catalytic role of ethnoracial division in the remaking of the state after the junking of the Fordist–Keynesian social compact and the collapse of the dark ghetto is analyzed in full in my book *Deadly Symbiosis: Race and the Rise of the Penal State* (Cambridge: Polity, 2015). The depth and rigidity of racial partition is a major factor behind the abyssal gap between the incarceration rates of the United States and of the European Union, just as it explains their divergent rates of poverty. See A. Alesina and E. L. Glaeser, *Fighting Poverty in the US and Europe: A World of Difference* (New York: Oxford University Press, 2004).

17 Foucault, *Surveiller et punir*; *Discipline and Punish*.

18 Foucault's writings on incarceration are dispersed and multifaceted, comprising some 60 texts written over 15 years, cutting across disciplinary domains and serving manifold purposes from the analytic to the political, and it is not possible to consider them in their richness and complexity here (these are captured by F. Boullant, *Michel Foucault et les prisons* [Paris: Presses Universitaires de France, 2003]). Instead, I focus on *Surveiller et punir*, owing to its canonical status in the study of punishment, deviance, and power (see, for instance, D. Garland, *Punishment and Society: A Study in Social Theory* [Chicago: University of Chicago Press, 1989], and J. Q. Whitman, "The Comparative Study of Criminal Punishment," *Annual Review of Law and Social Science* 1 [2005]: 17–34), entailing the common disregard of his later work on security and governmentality (P. O'Malley, "Governmental Criminology," in E. McLaughlin and T. Newburn, eds., *The Sage Handbook of Criminological Theory* (London: Sage, 2013), 319–36. Below, I give my own translation with page references to the original French edition, followed by the pagination in the US edition.

19 L. Wacquant, "Ordering Insecurity: Social Polarization and the Punitive Upsurge," *Radical Philosophy Review* 11, 1 (2008): 9–27.

20 Foucault, *Discipline and Punish*, 297–8.

21 T. Mathiesen, *Prison on Trial: A Critical Assessment* (London: Sage Publications, 1990).

22 This is particularly glaring in the California Department of Corrections, the country's second-largest carceral system after the Federal Bureau of Prisons, in which grotesque overcrowding (in 2008, the state packed 170,000 convicts in 33 prisons designed to hold 85,000) and systemic bureaucratic dysfunction combine to make a mockery of any pretense at "rehabilitation" (J. Petersilia, "California's Correctional Paradox of Excess and Deprivation," *Crime and Justice: A Review of Research* 37 [2008]: 207–78).

23 Foucault, *Discipline and Punish*, 301/294.

24 L. Wacquant, "Class, Race and Hyperincarceration in Revanchist America," *Daedalus*, thematic issue on "The Challenges of Mass Incarceration," 139, 3 (Summer 2010): 74–90.
25 L. Wacquant, *Prisons of Poverty* (Minneapolis: University of Minnesota Press, 2009).
26 Foucault, *Discipline and Punish*, 7.
27 *Ibid.*, 131.
28 G. Sykes, *The Society of Captives: A Study in a Maximum Security Prison* (Princeton: Princeton University Press, 1958/1974); G. Chantraine, *Par-delà les murs. Expériences et trajectoires en maison d'arrêt* (Paris: Presses Universitaires de France / Le Monde, 2004); and B. Crewe, *The Prisoner Society: Power, Adaptation and Social Life in an English Prison* (Oxford: Clarendon Press, 2009).
29 Foucault, *Discipline and Punish*, 298.
30 "Carceral circles widen and the prison form becomes gradually attenuated until it disappears... And finally this great carceral web joins all the disciplinary devices that operate disseminated across the society... The carceral archipelago transports this technique of the penal institution to the entire social body" (*ibid.*, 340). These errors and gaps in Foucault's conception of penal power and history are directly connected to his overly broad, vague, and discursivist conception of neoliberalism, picked up by later students of governmentality (see L. Wacquant, "Three Steps to a Historical Anthropology of Actually Existing Neoliberalism," *Social Anthropology* 20, 1 [January 2012]: 66–79; with responses by Johanna Bockman, Steve Collier, Daniel Goldstein, Mathieu Hilgers, Bob Jessop, Don Kalb, Jamie Peck and Nik Theodore [January–November 2012] for a more detailed critique).
31 Fox Piven and Cloward, *Regulating the Poor*.
32 D. Garland, *The Culture of Control: Crime and Social Order in Contemporary Society* (Chicago: University of Chicago Press, 2001).
33 L. Maurin and P. Savidan, *L'état des inégalités en France. Données et analyses* (Paris: Belin, 2008).
34 D. Grandquillot, *RSA. Revenu de solidarité active* (Paris: Gualino Editeur, 2009).
35 L. Bonelli, *La France a peur. Une histoire sociale de l'insécurité* (Paris: La Découverte, 2008).
36 Wacquant, "Ordering Insecurity."
37 B. Jessop, "Post-Fordism and the State," in A. Amin, ed., *Post-Fordism: A Reader* (Oxford: Basil Blackwell, 1994), 251–79; W. Streeck and K. Thelen, eds., *Beyond Continuity: Institutional Change in Advanced Political Economies* (Oxford: Oxford University Press, 2005); and J. D. Levy, ed., *The State After Statism: New*

State Activities in the Age of Liberalization (Cambridge, MA: Harvard University Press, 2006).

38 Garland, *The Culture of Control*, 165; emphasis added.

39 Wacquant, *Prisons of Poverty*, 87–102.

40 In a major comparative study of the linkages between penal policy and political economy in 12 contemporary capitalist countries, Cavadino and Dignan find that the nations they characterize as neoliberal (as distinct from conservative corporatist, social democratic, and oriental corporatist) are consistently more punitive and have become much more so in the past two decades. See M. Cavadino and J. Dignan, *Penal Systems: A Comparative Approach* (London: Sage Publications, 2006).

41 The international diffusion of "made in USA" penal categories and policies and its springs are treated at length in Wacquant, *Prisons of Poverty*, and "The Global Firestorm of Law and Order: On Neoliberalism and Punishment," *Thesis Eleven* 122 (Spring 2014): 72–88; see also the complementary argument of Andreas and Nadelmann stressing the pivotal role of the export of penality in foreign relations – P. Andreas and E. Nadelmann, *Policing the Globe: Criminalization and Crime Control in International Relations* (New York: Oxford University Press, 2006).

42 Garland, *The Culture of Control*, 77.

6

The Unfulfilled Promises of the Late Foucault and Foucauldian "Governmentality Studies"

Jan Rehmann

I will try to show that the late Foucault made interesting and promising announcements that neither he nor the Foucauldian "governmentality studies" ever realized. What Foucault promised was basically to distinguish between domination and power, between techniques of domination and of the self, and to investigate their interaction. I will evaluate both the potentials of the late Foucault's approach and its theoretical weaknesses. Focusing mainly on Foucault's 1977–8 lectures at the Collège de France, entitled *Security, Territory, Population*, as well as his 1978–9 lectures, *The Birth of Biopolitics*,[1] I will firstly demonstrate that Foucault did not stick to his own analytical distinctions and thus remained unable to conceptualize a cooperative power and agency from below; secondly, that his concept of "governmentality" covered a multitude of very different meanings so that it can hardly be put to work as an analytical concept; and finally, that he was unable to relate the "governmental" conceptions of leadership, in particular those of liberalism and neoliberalism, to the structures of social domination, in the framework of which they are continuously being developed and realized. This also applies to Foucauldian governmentality studies, which explicitly distanced themselves from any ideology critique, with the consequence that their interpretation of management literature tended to become a merely immanent retelling of neoliberal ideology without any critical distance. My main objection is that they failed to grasp the relationship between domination and subjection in neoliberalism. I propose to reinterpret their insights in a different framework: that is, the framework of a critical ideology theory.

Foucault's mediation of the techniques of domination and of the self

Foucault discovered the techniques of the self during the long and obviously crisis-ridden period between the first and second volumes of *The History of Sexuality*, i.e. between 1976 and 1984. Whereas, at the time of publication of *Discipline and Punish* in 1975, he had used the concept of power in the sense of a subtle and omnipresent formation of subjects that did not leave any room for subversion and resistance, he afterwards included the subjects' relationship to themselves. The way in which people organize their lives and the "techniques" they apply to themselves, to their attitudes, their bodies, and their psyche became an important component of Foucault's late concept of power. The exercise of power acknowledges others in principle as acting subjects in their own right, "having in front of them a field of possibility in which several conducts, several reactions, and various modes of behavior can take place,"[2] which includes the aspect of mutual influence and of the reversibility of power relations.[3] However, domination designates a "strategic" fixation, in which power relations are no longer reversible, but rather blocked and ossified (*bloquées et figées*).[4]

Unfortunately, Foucault did not carry through this distinction in a consistent fashion. In an interview in 1984, he was confronted with Hannah Arendt's distinction between a collective power, in which individuals gain a greater capacity to act than if they relied merely on themselves alone, and a power of domination, which might emerge from it or insert itself into it. Foucault responded that this is just a "verbal" distinction.[5] Furthermore, he usually did not distinguish between the two concepts analytically, according to qualitative dimensions, but rather quantitatively, according to the criterion of size and scale, so that "domination" described

the macrostructure and "power" described the microstructure. Whenever power became "global," he used the term
"domination," and whatever invaded and permeated immediate relationships was defined as "power."[6]

However, this is not a sustainable distinction. Domination,
which is formed around the ancient figure of the *dominus*
(*kyrios* [master]) and marks the intersection of patriarchal
and class rule, is also capable of permeating immediate
human relations, including the most intimate ones. A case in
point is patriarchal domination, whose ideological forms
and patterns are permanently internalized by both genders.
On the other hand, the altermondialist movements of the
World Social Forum aim to build a democratic and anti-
imperial power from below on a "global" level, and maintain
that it must not flip over again into a new form of uncontrolled domination. Foucault misses the opportunity to
re-conceptualize his concept of power from its etymological
roots (in Germanic and Romance languages) of ability/
capacity: the German term *Macht*, for example, goes back to
the Gothic *mahts* and *magan* ("to be capable"), which in turn
correspond to the French verb *pouvoir* that underlies the
Romance nouns *(le) pouvoir*, *(la) puissance*, and the Anglo-
Saxon *power*. Foucault's fascination with Nietzsche's elitist
will to power keeps preventing him from taking up Spinoza's
concept of power as a cooperative capacity to act (*potentia
agendi*).[7] The late Foucault's concept of power now includes
the aspects of self-conduct and techniques of the self, but it
does so in an individualistic manner, which fails to grasp the
potentials of collective agency and self-determination. It is at
this point that Foucault's "care of the self" merges with the
ideological conjuncture of neoliberalism.

But rather than focus on the weaknesses of Foucault's
approach, I would like to concentrate first on its possible
(though unrealized) strengths. Between the microstructure of
potentially reciprocal power relations and the fixated blocks
of domination, Foucault assumed an intermediary level which
he called "governmentality."[8] He defined the term as a
"conduct of conducts." The expression is based on an ambiguity of the French verb *conduire*, which signifies on the one
hand "directing" someone (*conduire quelqu'un*), on the other
hand the way in which one conducts oneself (*se conduit*),

comports oneself, or behaves, so that governmentality means "*conduire des conduits*" – conducting people's conduct.[9]

The distinction between techniques of domination and of the self enabled Foucault to develop a better sense of subtle forms of resistance, which did not yet play a role in *Discipline and Punish* and the first volume of *The History of Sexuality* – namely, revolts of conduct articulated in the will "to be conducted differently" or "to escape direction by others and to define the way for each to conduct himself."[10] An example of such "insubordination" (*insoumission*) or "counter-conduct" was medieval asceticism, which Foucault described as an "exercise of self on self... in which the authority, presence and gaze of someone else is, if not impossible, at least unnecessary." It is a "reversed obedience" or "excess," by which certain themes of religious experience are utilized against the structures of power;[11] the religious communities are in part based on the "refusal of the pastor's authority and its theological or ecclesiological justifications," replacing the clergy–laity dimorphism by "relationships of reciprocal obedience," or the priesthood of all believers;[12] in mysticism, the soul is not offered to the other for examination by a system of confessions, but "sees itself in God and... God in itself" and thereby short-circuits the pastoral hierarchy by replacing it with an immediate communication.[13] Another movement of counter-conduct is the return to Scripture;[14] eschatological beliefs disqualify the pastor's role by claiming that the times are by themselves in the process of being fulfilled.[15] Another case in point is the truth-speech (*parrhesia*) of ancient Cynicism, which manifests itself as an "interpellation of the powerful in the form of the diatribe."[16]

The concept of "conducting conduct" could indeed open up promising research questions. Obviously, the conduct of life under contradictory conditions is a complex and complicated affair. One has to balance different demands, prioritize them, bring them into a linear temporal sequence – a procedure which cannot be achieved without a certain degree of critical evaluation of the necessities of life and of self-discipline.[17] To the extent that an instance of domination or a superordinated ideological power successfully connects with these strategies of self-conduct, speaks in their name, and mobilizes them for certain purposes, it gains access to the structures of common sense and thus finds a sounding board so strong that intellectual criticism is unable to counter it. Conversely, communities and individuals can only resist ideological socialization, in a sustainable manner, if they develop and practice capacities of collective and individual self-conduct.

It seems as if the late Foucault had adopted a Gramscian concept of leadership or hegemony which, in contrast to violence, contains an aspect of consensus. His claim to mediate techniques of domination and of the self touches upon a central issue of bourgeois hegemony, namely the active and voluntary subordination to domination. The desire to explain the efficacy and appeal of such a subordination, which is experienced as free and responsible subjectivity, was the founding impulse of the ideology theories that emerged in the 1970s and 1980s, first in connection with Louis Althusser in France, then with Stuart Hall in the UK and the *Projekt Ideologietheorie* (PIT) in Berlin. Foucault's problematic of how the techniques of domination and of the self are interconnected would then be located in what ideology theories usually discuss in terms of an encounter of the ideological and common-sense practices. His specific contribution would be the analysis of ideological patterns and self-conducts as particular technologies of power and their assemblage as a hegemonic bloc, which is effectuated as a "conduct of conducts."

But, of course, Foucault and the governmentality studies claim to have left the concepts of hegemony and ideology far behind. Both Stuart Hall and Pierre Bourdieu are criticised for being stuck in the "old paradigm" of ideology critique and for ignoring the fact that neoliberalism's leadership techniques must be investigated in a "positive" way.[18] In the course of this abandonment of ideology critique, the promises of investigating the interactions of techniques of domination and of the self drop out of sight as well.

The enigmatic content of the concept of governmentality

The problem starts with the term "governmentality" itself, which sparkles in all directions and whose floating meanings can hardly be determined. The French neologism seems to carry an enigmatic content which dissipates as soon as one translates it into plain language. If one tries to explain it by its two components "government" and "mentality," one gets something like the "mentality of (the) government," or perhaps a way to reflect on government.[19] However, this explanation was contradicted by Michel Sennelart, the editor of Foucault's lectures at the Collège de France, who proclaimed that the term is not derived from the noun "mentality," but emerged from the adjective *gouvernemental* being transformed into a noun, in the same way as *musicalité* can be derived from *musical*.[20] If this is accurate (Sennelart does not provide any philological proof), one could ask all the more whether the new terminological coinage is really worth the effort: taking the adjective *gouvernemental*, which is itself derived from the noun *gouvernement*, and then retransforming it into another noun by adding the new ending *-ité*, does not yield anything more than "government-like" or "of the kind of government," which again does not have any explanatory power.

More importantly, Foucault uses the term in very different ways: on the most general level, "governmentality" designates "the way in which one conducts the conducts" of people[21] – that is to say, the "conducting of conducts," which by its consensual components is "different from 'reigning or ruling,' and not the same as 'commanding' or 'laying down the law,' or being a sovereign, suzerain, lord," but instead is enacted as "government of souls."[22]

On a second level, it describes a "line of force" that traverses the history of the West and leads to the preeminence of "government" over all other types of power.[23] It is the "pastorate" of the Jewish-Christian tradition, i.e. a particular conception of leadership that understands itself in terms of the relationship of a shepherd to his flock, and has its origin "in the East and in the Hebrews."[24] According to Foucault, this concept of leadership was foreign to Greek thought. However, this is an assumption, which was already challenged by his own counter-examples, according to which the King is addressed 44 times as "shepherd" by the *Iliad* and 12 times by the *Odyssey*;[25] the Pythagoreans derived from *nomeus*, the shepherd, the *nomos*, the law, and the title of Zeus as *Nomios*, the god-shepherd.[26] In Plato's *Critias*, *The*

Republic, and *The Laws*, the good magistrate is seen as a good shepherd.[27] Plato's *Statesman* applies the shepherd-metaphor to the political leader as well. However, this is subsequently revealed as insufficient, because the specifics of the politician's activity must be grasped according to the model of "weaving": just as the weaver joins the warp and the weft, the statesman binds together the "virtues in their different forms," and "different contrasting temperaments."[28] Foucault's account is accurate, but the example does not demonstrate what he claims it does. Instead of proving that the shepherd–flock relationship is foreign to "Greek thought," it shows, as Foucault himself admits, that Plato was critically scrutinizing "if not a commonplace, then at least a familiar opinion."[29] But, of course, this common sense coincides with what Foucault portrays as "Greek thought." Whereas Foucault confronted the "oriental" figure of the shepherd with the Greek concept of the King as the "good pilot," who governs not primarily individuals but the "ship" of the city-state,[30] a philological evaluation published in the *Reallexikon für Antike und Christentum* came to the conclusion that Hesiode, Aeschylus, Sophocles, and Euripides also applied the title of shepherd "to military leaders, e.g. to captains of ships."[31] Foucault's assumption of an originally "Oriental" concept of the pastorate is itself what one could describe, using Edward Said, as an "orientalist" conception. A study of social history could have shown him that stockbreeding (and thereby the figure of the shepherd) was widespread throughout the entire Mediterranean area (and beyond), not only in its "Eastern" parts.

On a third level, the term "political governmentality" covers a period that starts with the Reformation and Counter-Reformation in the sixteenth century – which also sees the transition to large-territory states – and, in the first half of the seventeenth century, coincides with the emergence of *raison d'Etat*.[32] Foucault is mainly interested in the way the ancient understanding of governing the polis merged with the Christian concept of the shepherd, and how the Christian pastorate became increasingly secularized and reached into everyday life. However, the conceptions of leadership belonging to this type of governmentality – like mercantilism, cameralistics, *raison d'Etat*, "Polizeiwissenschaft," and Physiocrats

– were still blocked by the predominance of the power of sovereignty, so that "the art of government could not find its own dimension."[33]

This concentration on the state was only overcome in the middle of the eighteenth century by the "liberal" art of government, which in Foucault's account opens up the period of "modern governmental reason."[34] It is only in the framework of this fourth meaning that it became "possible to think, reflect, and calculate the problem of government outside the juridical framework of sovereignty."[35] What we had learned so far were obviously merely precursors of governmentality, and, indeed, Foucault proclaims: "We live in the era of a governmentality discovered in the eighteenth century."[36] But even this relatively narrow usage of the term still covers an enormously complex array, containing multiple formations as varied as liberalism, conservatism, fascism, social democracy, and administrative state-socialism, and it remains unclear on what grounds the governmentality studies can claim to have found an analytical key for the specific understanding of neoliberalism.

One therefore arrives at four different meanings of "governmentality," which in Foucault's usage continuously flow into each other: leadership in general as "a kind of basic condition of human societies";[37] an "oriental" and then "Jewish-Christian" pastorate permeating the culture of the West; political governmentality from the sixteenth century onwards; and liberal governmentality from the eighteenth century onwards. It seems as if Foucault tried in ever new attempts to approach an abstract concept of governmentality to history, without ever arriving at a concrete historical or sociological constellation.

However, it is not only the concept's scope that oscillates, but also the level of reality to which it is referring. Whereas the power of sovereignty until (and including) Machiavelli had the "territory" and its inhabitants as a target and, in a "circular relationship," had its aim in itself, the "government," from La Perrière's *Le miroir politique* (1555) onwards, was related "to a sort of complex of men and things," "the intrication of men and things": people involved with wealth, resources, the means of subsistence, etc.[38] But this cannot be the definition of a modern, economical type of governmentality, because people were always bound up with "things," and all domination had to relate to this connection – for example, to the disposal of natural resources, the labor-force, the economic infrastructure, and so on. Did Foucault believe in earnest that such a disposal was a modern invention, whereas the rulers of pre-modern times were only interested in "territory" and increasing their power as such? This would indeed be an ideological fairytale, in which the entire complex of the relations of production, reproduction, and distribution, of the imperial control of raw materials, of the exploitation and over-taxation of subjugated peoples, was dissimulated. How long could the Roman emperors have entertained the Roman *plebs* with "bread and circuses" if the provinces had successfully stopped their grain deliveries for an extended time?

Foucault tried to evade such critical questions by changing the level of argumentation: by the "art of government" he does not mean "the way in which governors really governed," but rather "the reasoned way of governing best and...reflection on the best possible way of governing."[39] According to this statement, "governmentality" is not about real practices of leadership and hegemony, but about certain patterns of reflection laid down in guide-books. Such a limitation could indeed be a useful methodological decision. The phenomenological reconstruction of leadership concepts could become an important component of an "immanent critique" which confronts ideologies with their own "truth," or, in Adorno's words, "what a society presents itself as being with what it actually is."[40]

But such a self-limitation, in turn, is in contradiction with Foucault's definition of governmentality as "the ensemble formed by institutions, procedures, analyses and reflections, calculations, and tactics that allow the exercise of this very specific, albeit very complex, power that has the population as its target, political economy as its major form of knowledge, and apparatuses of security as its essential technical instrument."[41] The ensemble of institutions, practices, and interpretative patterns in a certain historical period would in turn constitute the classical object of an ideology-theoretical research program. But the promised research is never realized. Foucault again delivers glossy menus announcing delicious dishes, but the readers never get anything to eat.

The theoretical flimsiness can be studied with the example of liberalism. Foucault claims to analyze liberalism neither as a theory, nor as an ideology, but rather "as a practice, that is to say, a 'way of doing things' directed toward objectives and regulating itself by continuous reflection."[42] But this is exactly not what he is actually doing. Instead of dealing with the practices and accompanying reflections of liberalism, he confines himself to the view that liberalism "constitutes...a tool for the criticism of reality," "a form of critical reflection" on previous or present varieties of governmentality, in particular a critique of excessive government and a concept of governmental self-limitation.[43] Foucault's definitions coincide entirely with the ideological self-image of liberalism, which likes to imagine itself as a philosophy and politics that stand in opposition to state regulation, and thereby represses the fact that in real history it manifested itself until the late nineteenth century primarily as a "possessive individualism" aiming at the maintenance of bourgeois property relations, and frequently did so with the violent and disciplinary measures of the repressive state apparatuses.

Foucault's paradigm, which is often hailed in secondary literature because of its superannuation of "ideology critique," does not allow us to grasp the ideological function of liberalism in the framework of bourgeois relations of domination. His account uncritically identifies with the object and remains on the level of an intuitive and empathetic retelling.[44] This also applies to his interpretation of neoliberalism. Since the economic and social developments and the political relations of force drop out of his interpretative framework, he is unable, as Tilman Reitz observes, "to establish a sustainable position towards his object": the neoliberal theories seem to emerge out of nothing and to find acceptance without any motivation – the reasons for their importance and success remain obscure.[45]

If it seemed at first that the late Foucault approached the Gramscian problematic of hegemony, it becomes clear now that this was merely a rhetorical gesture. Whereas Gramsci tried to grasp the connections between leadership and domination, hegemony and force, *società civile* and *società politica*, Foucault's account made the overall framework of bourgeois domination and the repressive armor of ideological practices disappear into thin air. The promised investigation of the connection between the techniques of domination and of the self got lost in the immanent reproduction of liberalism's ideological self-understanding. Foucault's concept of "governmentality" thus loses its critical edge on both sides: as it obfuscates capitalist domination, it also severs the aspect of self-conduct and self-techniques from the perspective of collective agency and struggles for social justice, and narrows them down to a neoliberal "do-it-yourself" of ideology.[46]

Those who, for whatever reason, decide to adopt and work with the artificial neologism of "governmentality" should at least bring themselves to address and to overcome its ambiguity: either one uses the term as a synonym for a materialist concept of the ideological – which would, however, mean that one actually investigates the ensemble of ideological powers, practices, and thought-forms of a specific period – or one employs it in a more modest sense, which also corresponds to the operational usage of Foucault – that is, in the sense of leadership strategies, *inasmuch as* and *how* they are reflected in certain types of guide-books: as the "reflexive prism"[47] of a hegemonic project. However, this would mean that one must not confuse such a textual representation with the entire ensemble of the ideological. Intellectual honesty would require that one resists the temptation to blow it up into an alternative to ideology critique and ideology theory.

Eliminating the inner contradictions of neoliberal ideology

This leads me to Foucauldian governmentality studies and its interpretation of neoliberalism, which I will mainly discuss using the example of the works of Ulrich Bröckling and Sven Opitz.[48] To a large extent, their readers learn what they could acquire anyway from the statements of entrepreneurs, from management literature, government proclamations, and the mainstream press: that we are all called upon to take the initiative in our jobs, that customer service is all that counts, that each of us needs to be our own entrepreneur – personally responsible, creative, and flexible, etc. In between, the authors insert some Foucauldian terms like the "pastoral" model of leadership, the "hermeneutics of desire," the indefatigable will to knowledge, etc., which serve as gestures to signify some sort of theoretical "distance." But this is a simulation. The evaluation basically amounts to the assumption that neoliberal "governmentality" should be characterized by the mobilization of capacities for self-conduct. This does little more than translate the overall rhetoric of activation in the management literature into a theoretical discourse. There is hardly any indication of the real place, relevance, and function of these highly ideological texts within the actual culture of enterprises, or in the general framework of neoliberal domination and its leadership methods. The approach thus shares the "destiny of a shadow-boxer who never gets hold of his opponent."[49]

Some examples might illustrate how governmentality studies fails to keep a critical distance from the advertising language of the neoliberal management literature and guidebooks they try to get a hold on. So-called "total quality management," which endeavors to apply quality control to all activities of the enterprise and to put the orientation toward the customer above everything else, is characterized by Bröckling as follows: quality is now determined by the "principle of prophylaxis," it obtains a "pro-active" character and a "preventive orientation." The idea behind these glittering words is basically that mistakes of production or service are to be prevented beforehand, instead of being corrected afterwards.[50] However, such a concern is, at least on this level of generality, not in the least a new achievement – it would apply to the assembly-line as well. Quality is "no goal," but rather a "process that never ends" – not a result, but an "action-parameter," reports Bröckling.[51] But this is obviously a nonsensical assumption: quality is of course still a "goal," and a "result" as well, or else clients would immediately return the product or complain about the unsatisfactory service. Since Bröckling believes he has left ideology critique far behind, he is not interested in (or capable of) revealing the abuse of language by an advertisement discourse, which tries to sell its "products" in the brightest colors as the newest and most revolutionary development. The more social theory gives in to such advertisement language, the less prepared it becomes for identifying what is really new.[52]

Bröckling goes on to assume that the requirement of focusing entirely on the client has replaced the "factory rules of the disciplinary era," which still insisted on punctuality, diligence, and order.[53] This coincides with Opitz's assumption that neoliberal leadership technologies are "post-disciplinary."[54] But can such a transposition really be maintained? What happens when a worker or employee does not arrive on time – for example, when meeting a client? More "flexibility" and more flexible working hours do not at all imply that the products of labor do not need to be delivered at a pre-given (or negotiated) time. This can even be gathered from neoliberal discourse itself: since *"lean production"* is (among other things) about the reduction of stock levels and storage-time, its *"just in time* principle" proclaims punctual delivery as an absolute requirement –otherwise the subcontractor might immediately lose its contract. Instead of declaring the era of discipline to be over and to have been replaced by the era of client-orientation and self-conduct, it would be more productive to look for specific forms of disciplinary demands under the conditions of computerized labor in high-tech capitalism. It is symptomatic that some of the substantial investigations of neoliberal management go back again to Foucault's former concept of disciplinary power.[55]

When Bröckling reports that subjectivity was for the Taylorist era nothing but a "factor of disturbance" that needed to be controlled,[56] this is again a misleading statement.[57] It underestimates how Fordism, through its puritan campaigns, and its education in hygiene and morality, as well as through its compensating family-ideologies, engendered a highly intense formation of subjectivities. According to Gramsci, it was even "the biggest collective effort to date to create, with unprecedented speed, and with a consciousness of purpose unmatched in history, a new type of worker and of man"[58] – a finding that could well be combined with Foucault's thesis of a "productive" constitution of the modern *dispositif* of sexuality. What should be investigated is how, in the transition to a high-tech mode of production and at the crossroads of labor conditions, education, mass culture, and ideological socialization, subjectivities are generated in a new way.

Bröckling informs us of *kaizen*, a Japanese term for "improvement," or "change for the better," signifying a critical search for amelioration, in which employees engage in a common diagnosis of mistakes and shortcomings – without moralizing or looking for "culprits": "In order to investigate and to overcome mistakes, these need to be laid open without any fear of sanctions."[59] It is indeed an interesting phenomenon that, in its efforts to enhance labor productivity, neoliberal management literature is compelled to take up elements that could be part of a "horizontal" communication. We encounter a similar phenomenon in the internet, which is, as a network, "horizontally" designed, and at the same time exposed to verticalization by corporations (and, of course, to systematic spying) – it is "anarchic and nevertheless reproduces relations of domination."[60] Unfortunately, Bröckling does not investigate the contradictions that emerge whenever such seemingly "horizontal" interpellations collide with the hierarchical realities of capitalist enterprises: how could an anxiety-free discussion of mistakes be possible in the context of mass unemployment and job insecurity, in which every revelation of errors can become a personal survival risk? Engaging in a "communication free of domination"[61] would in principle require new relations of economic democracy. Under capitalist conditions, it can only be realized in a restricted and partial manner, and is only realistic amongst privileged sections of the labor process, where the demand for qualified workers is high and jobs are secure.

Bröckling describes the so-called "360-degree-evaluation," by which every employee is exposed to the anonymous judgment of all the others, as a "democratic panopticism," a "non-hierarchical model of reciprocal visibility, in which everyone is both the observer of all the others and the observed by all the others."[62] This description is, however, naïve and misleading, because it severs the form of evaluation from the surrounding asymmetrical power relations of the enterprise. An ideology-theoretical analysis would instead be interested, firstly, in the way the results of such an evaluation can be utilized for promotions, transfers, or dismissals; and secondly, how the mere possibility of such a utilization impacts back on relationships among the workforce and enhances attitudes that mobilize the employees against each other and against their own cooperative interests. According to Peterson, in his experience the 360-degree-evaluation had the effect that "the interactions with the colleagues were superimposed by...tactical considerations and prevented the development of relations of friendship."[63] The assumption of a "flattening of the panoptic asymmetry"[64] dissimulates the development of a vertical panopticism which, based on electronic surveillance and network technologies, by far exceeds what Foucault analyzed in *Discipline and Punish*. According to the American Management Association, about 75 percent of employees in the private sector are subjected to electronic-surveillance monitoring, which is for Stephen Gill, who reports this, one of the characteristics that justify speaking of a "disciplinary neoliberalism."[65]

In their eagerness to renounce ideology critique and to focus instead on "positive" leadership techniques, governmentality studies authors establish an intuitive and empathetic relationship to the management programs they claim to analyze. Since they do not investigate their ideological functions and functioning in the framework of neoliberal high-tech capitalism, they have no methodological instrument to distinguish between real new patterns of hegemonic leadership, on the one hand, and made-up fantasies and empty rhetoric on the other. Above all, they reproduce the view of management which looks at employees from the perspective of managerial leaders and dissimulates the domination and alienation in neoliberal capitalism behind the smokescreen of motivational incentives and appeals to teamwork.

Opitz comes to the conclusion that neoliberal leadership techniques aim at enhancing capacities of self-governance and favor an "extremely loose coupling" of power relations, which "under no circumstances may turn into a relation of domination."[66] He even indulges in the stylistic howler that neoliberal leaders are supposed to withdraw in a "post-heroic" way, in order to open up a space where the employees "can constitute a subjective desire."[67] Such evaluations are deeply stuck in neoliberal ideology. A critical ideology theory would instead look at the outer arrangement of the social order: the neoliberal interpellations aiming at the mobilization of capacities of "self-conduct" operate within specific relations of domination, are limited by them, and can only be grasped in their functioning within this comprehensive framework.

A problematic equation of subjectivation and subjection

It was not just the techniques of domination, however, that dropped out of sight for governmentality studies. It does not look any better regarding self-conduct: since its interpretation is restricted to the programmatic interpellations of management literature without investigating their encounter with real subjects, the distinction between techniques of self-conduct and of domination becomes obsolete.[68]

That governmentality studies dropped Foucault's initial claim to distinguish between domination and self-conduct is primarily due to the fact that they adopted a subject-theory which – often via Judith Butler – equates the emergence of a subject and its subjection, of *subjectivation* and *subjection/assujetissment*.[69] What Judith Butler describes as a "postliberatory insight"[70] can be traced back to Lacanian psychoanalysis, according to which the constitution of a subject coincides with its subordination under the "law of language." Althusser adopted and integrated this equation in his concept of ideology in general. In a way, Judith Butler deepened the anthropological level of explanation by introducing a "founding submission" which readies the subject "to be compelled by the authoritative interpellation."[71] These interpretations are based on an ahistorical construction that can be seen already in Freud's psychoanalytical theory: a dichotomy between "society" and "individual" whereby the former is necessarily "repressive" and the desires of the individuals are conceived beforehand as "non-societal." This arrangement establishes an "un-societal foundational structure" of the individual and makes it impossible to conceptualize the formation of self-determined capacities to act.[72]

Such an "anthropological" foundation has far-reaching consequences for the analyses of governmentality studies: if it is determined beforehand that subjectivity and subjection/ submission are by definition one and the same, it comes as no surprise that Foucault's differentiation between technologies of the self and of domination cannot be maintained, and that the self-conduct of individuals and their ideological integration into the *dispositif* of neoliberalism cannot be analytically distinguished. This is the systematic reason why the analysis of neoliberal leadership techniques loses its critical edge: by removing the contradictions of socialization under the antagonistic conditions of neoliberal capitalism, governmentality studies can no longer identify where and how neoliberalism takes up and hijacks emancipatory elements of self-socialization and self-conduct and integrates them in a modernized system of bourgeois hegemony.

The renunciation of analytical distinctions not only overlooks the contradictory dialectics of neoliberal socialization, it also impedes the development of a sustainable concept of resistance. For Opitz, resistance is only conceivable as a "border attitude" (*Grenzhaltung*), an "operation at the margins" (*Randgang*), or a "line of escape" (*Fluchtlinie*), which does no more than complement the *techne* of government.[73] "Resistance" is thus necessarily restricted to small tactical displacements within the framework of domination and its hegemonic ideologies. Any attempt to formulate a "global alternative to the existing conditions" is denounced as an illusory fallacy, because it would mean becoming entrapped in the utopian concept of subject liberation so convincingly criticized by Foucault.[74] This corresponds to a notion of critique that needs to become as flexible as its objects and therefore has to renounce any "standpoint."[75]

It very much looks as if governmentality studies tries to provide the existing dispersion and helplessness of social movements and the Left *vis-à-vis* neoliberal hegemony with a theoretical justification. Instead of looking for strategies to overcome its weaknesses, it confirms and naturalizes them. What this theoretical framework makes systematically inconceivable is the possibility of finding new coalescing points (like the Occupy Wall Street movement) or new types of connective parties (like Syriza and Podemos) that could become stepping-stones for building a counter-hegemony from below which is able to reclaim and reappropriate the elements of self-conduct that were hijacked and alienated by neoliberalism.

Toward an ideology-theoretical reinterpretation of governmentality studies

My theoretical criticism does not imply that governmentality studies is without interest. By scrutinizing management literature for new leadership concepts, they are dealing with a relevant, if partial, section of neoliberal ideologies. Their main methodological mistake is, similarly to Foucault, that they elevate the presentation of neoliberal self-description to an overall "theory" and declare it to be an alternative to ideology critique and ideology theory. It is precisely by this overblown claim that a potentially useful phenographic reconstruction turns into a theoretical impasse, which plunges the dimensions both of domination and of self-socialization into a gray, "postliberatory" fog. The interesting question is therefore, whether and how such a cul-de-sac could be avoided by a critical ideology theory.

With regard to such a critical reinterpretation, I would like to confine myself to three tentative theses:

1   Although there is much talk in governmentality studies about "techniques" and "technologies" (of power or of government), the authors are usually not interested in the technological development of computerized labor. I think the new leadership techniques proposed in management literature should be related to the mode of production in high-tech capitalism. When Gramsci described the "forced elaboration of a new type of man" in Fordism, he conceptualized it as a "psycho-physical adaptation to the new industrial structure."[76] Accordingly, the neoliberal leadership technologies are not just new "constructions," but should be investigated as an integral part of the rapid transformations in the mode of production. What is new, for example, is that competition now invades the relations between singular departments of an enterprise, so that the limits of corporations are perforated by multiple commodity–money relations.[77] What governmentality

studies portray as a shift toward "self-conduct" is then revealed as part of a contradictory subject form in which individuals are interpellated as autonomous subjects and at the same time kept in subalternity: self-responsibility, but for alien property; autonomy as self-subjection under one's own marketability.[78]

2   Whereas governmentality studies establish an extremely homogeneous model in which the discourse of self-activation seems to spread throughout the entire society without hindrance and inflection, an ideology-theoretical approach would analyze new leadership techniques in relation to the social divisions of neoliberal capitalism. Whoever watched Ken Loach's film *Bread and Roses*, about the Mexican working poor in San Francisco, or read Barbara Ehrenreich's classic book *Nickel and Dimed*,[79] about the low-wage sector in the United States, might have experienced some difficulties in identifying the subtle techniques of self-conduct, but would have encountered overwhelming characteristics of an outspoken "despotism of capital."[80] However, for Bröckling, such a despotism is no more than a phenomenon of the past, long since overcome.[81]

The alleged homogeneous efficacy of the neoliberal discourse of self-conduct results from a twofold methodological abstraction. Firstly, governmentality studies overlook the fact that neoliberal class divides also translate into different strategies of subjection: on the one hand, "positive" motivation, the social integration of different milieus, manifold offers on the therapy market; on the other hand, the build-up of a huge prison system, surveillance, and police control. The former is mainly directed toward the middle classes and some "qualified" sections of the working class; the latter mainly toward the "dangerous classes."[82] According to Robert Castel, today's power is defined by a management that carefully anticipates social splits and cleavages: "The emerging tendency is to assign different social destinies to individuals in line with their varying capacity to live up to the requirements of competitiveness and profitability."[83]

Secondly, governmentality studies do not take into account the fact that even similar neoliberal interpellations may have different and even opposite effects in different "milieus": the appeals to creativity and initiative might play a supportive and constructive role in the formation of identities if they correlate to labor conditions that actually require and bolster a certain (relative) autonomy and freedom; they tend to destroy agency and subjectivities if there are no, or very restricted, alternative possibilities to act. Neoliberal interpellations of "empowerment" then have the effect of confirming the individual's lack of capabilities and "worthlessness." What Bourdieu analyzed as the "destiny-effect" among contingent laborers and marginalized youngsters[84] can be seen as the dark flip-side of the neoliberal interpellations of self-mobilization and creativity. A complementary ideological effect could be described as the illusory "opiate" of the excluded and marginalized: as Loïc Wacquant shows in his study of a Chicago ghetto, the interviewees all gave the same completely unrealistic, but honestly believed, statement that they would enrol in a college in the near future.[85]

3   Finally, governmentality studies need to be reinterpreted on the basis of a subject theory that takes seriously the agency of individuals, and their attempts at self-socialization and self-conduct. The emergence of capacities to act is not to be equated beforehand with subjection.[86] Of course, this does not mean falling back on an "essentialist" approach, which invokes the ahistorical notion of a benign and joyful "essence" slumbering within humans, just waiting to emerge in a society without classes and state domination. Over and again, alternative and emancipatory movements are confronted with the task of distinguishing between aspects of alienated socialization and of cooperative self-determination – not once and for all, but ever anew in a given concrete conjuncture. A critical ideology theory needs to grasp the contradictions between neoliberal discourses of self-activation and the submission to alienated relations of domination. It also needs the support of a subject-theory that is able to distinguish between neoliberalism's attractive promises of individualization and its practical reductionism, which degrades freedom and individuality to private and egoistical forms of "possessive individualism."

Only with the help of such recurring and ever-new distinctions will it be possible to confront the hegemonic crisis of neoliberal capitalism, to break the appeal of neoliberal ideologies, and to build a democratic-socialist counter-hegemony from below.

Notes

1 M. Foucault, *Security, Territory, Population: Lectures at the Collège de France, 1977–1978*, trans. Graham Burchell (New York: Palgrave Macmillan, 2007), and *The Birth of Biopolitic: Lectures at the Collège de France, 1978–1979*, trans. Graham Burchell (London: Palgrave Macmillan, 2008).
2 M. Foucault, *Dits et écrits*, vol. II, *1976–1988* (Paris: Quarto Gallimard, 2001), 1056.
3 *Ibid.*, 2061.
4 *Ibid.*, 1062, 1529.
5 *Ibid.*, 1408.
6 *Ibid.*, 1062, 1529.
7 For a comparison of Spinoza's *potentia agendi* as a cooperative power from below and Nietzsche's verticalist and ultimately exterminist *will to power*, see J. Rehmann, *Postmoderner Links-Nietzscheanismus. Deleuze & Foucault. Eine Dekonstruktion* (Hamburg: Argument-Verlag, 2004), 52–60; for Foucault's adoption of Nietzsche's combination of "will to truth" and "will to power," see *ibid.*, 117–20.
8 "There are three levels of my analysis of power: the strategic relations, the techniques of government, and the techniques of domination that are applied to the others and to the techniques of the self" (*ibid.*, 1547); "What I call 'governmentality' is the encounter between the techniques of domination applied to the others and the techniques of the self" (*ibid.*, 1604). Cf. T. Lemke, *Eine Kritik der politischen Vernunft: Foucaults Analyse der modernen Gouvernementalität* (Hamburg: Argument-Verlag, 1997), 264, 308–9.
9 See Foucault, *Dits et écrits*, vol. II, *1976–1988*, 1056, 1401; Foucault, *Security, Territory, Population*, 193.
10 Foucault, *Security, Territory, Population*, 194–5.
11 *Ibid.*, 200–1, 204, and 207–8.
12 *Ibid.*, 208, 210–11.
13 *Ibid.*, 212.
14 *Ibid.*, 213.
15 *Ibid.*, 214.

16 M. Foucault, *The Government of Self and Others: Lectures at the Collège de France, 1982–1983*, trans. G. Burchell (New York: Palgrave Macmillan, 2010), 344.

17 For a Marxist analysis of the contradictions of everyday life in a capitalist society, see K. Holzkamp, "Alltägliche Lebensführung als subjektwissenschaftliches Grundkonzept," *Das Argument*, 212, 37 (1995): 817–46.

18 See A. Barry, O. Thomas, and N. Rose, eds., *Foucault and Political Reason: Liberalism, Neo-Liberalism and Rationalities of Government* (Chicago: University of Chicago Press, 1996), 11, and U. Bröckling, "Totale Mobilmachung. Menschenführung im Qualitäts- und Selbstmanagement," in U. Bröckling, S. Krasmann, and T. Lemke, eds., *Gouvernementalität der Gegenwart: Studien zur Ökonomisierung des Sozialen* (Frankfurt am Main: Suhrkamp, 2000), 19. To assume that Bourdieu's critique of neoliberalism amounts to a "defense of the state" (*ibid.*) is, of course, a misleading simplification: Bourdieu was aiming at a democratically controlled finance sector and also at an alliance with fractions of the social state – not only on a national level, but in a European framework.

19 M. Dean, "The way we think about government," in Dean, *Governmentality: Power and Rule in Modern Society* (London: Sage Publications, 1999), 16ff.; and see Bröckling, "Totale Mobilmachung," 8; S. Opitz, *Gouvernementalität im Postfordismus: Macht, Wissen und Techniken des Selbst im Feld unternehmerischer Rationalität* (Hamburg: Argument-Verlag, 2004), 60; and S. Opitz, "Gouvernementalität im Postfordismus. Zur Erkundung unternehmerischer Steuerungsregime der Gegenwart," in C. Kaindl, ed., *Subjekte im Neoliberalismus* (Marburg: BdWi-Verlag, 2007), 96–7.

20 In Foucault, *Security, Territory, Population*, 399–40 n.126.

21 Foucault, *The Birth of Biopolitics*, 186.

22 Cf. Foucault, *Security, Territory, Population*, 115–16, 121, 192.

23 *Ibid.*, 108.

24 *Ibid.*, 123, 147, 364.

25 *Ibid.*, 136ff.

26 *Ibid.*, 137.

27 *Ibid.*, 138.

28 *Ibid.*, 145–6.

29 *Ibid.*, 141–2.

30 *Ibid.*, 123.

31 J. Engemann, "Hirt" ["shepherd"], in E. Dassmann et al., eds., *Reallexikon für Antike und Christentum* (Stuttgart: Anton Hiersemann Verlag, 1991 [1950–]), vol. XV, 580.

32 Foucault, *Security, Territory, Population*, 364.

33 *Ibid.*, 102–3.

34 Foucault, *The Birth of Biopolitics*, 11, 13, 20.

35 Foucault, *Security, Territory, Population*, 104.

36 *Ibid.*, 109.

37 Bröckling, Krasmann, and Lemke, eds., *Gouvernementalität der Gegenwart*, 18.

38 Foucault, *Security, Territory, Population*, 96–7.

39 Foucault, *The Birth of Biopolitics*, 2.

40 T. L. W. Adorno, *Gesammelte Schriften*, 20 volumes, ed. R. Tiedemann (Frankfurt am Main: Suhrkamp, 1973–86), vol. VIII, 347.

41 Foucault, *Security, Territory, Population*, 108.

42 Foucault, *The Birth of Biopolitics*, 318.

43 *Ibid.*, 320–3.

44 Gordon explains Foucault's distance from Marxism and anarchism by his fascination for liberalism: "Foucault does seem to have been (at least) intrigued by the properties of liberalism as a form of knowledge calculated to limit power," in C. Gordon, "Introduction," in G. Burchell, C. Gordon, and P. Miller, eds., *The Foucault Effect: Studies in Governmentality*, 1–51 (Chicago: University of Chicago Press, 1991), 47.

45 T. Reitz, "Neoliberalismus in Staat und Geist," *Das Argument*, 261, 47, 3 (2005): 373.

46 W. F. Haug, *Elemente einer Theorie des Ideologischen* (Hamburg: Argument-Verlag, 1993), 172, 227.

47 Foucault, *Security, Territory, Population*, 276.

48 Bröckling, "Totale Mobilmachung," and "Jeder könnte, aber nicht alle können. Konturen des unternehmerischen Selbst," *Mittelweg*, 36, 11 (2002), Heft 4 (www.eurozine.com/article/2002-10-02-broeckling-de.html); Opitz, *Gouvernementalität im Postfordismus*, and "Gouvernementalität im Postfordismus."

49 T. Reitz and S. Draheim, "Schattenboxen im Neoliberalismus. Kritik und Perspektiven der deutschen Foucault-Rezeption," in Kaindl, ed., *Subjekte im Neoliberalismus*, 119.

50 Bröckling, "Totale Mobilmachung," 136–7.

51 *Ibid.*, 137.

52 Frigga Haug's analysis of Peter Hartz's *Job Revolution*, which reveals the discursive strategy of a "ruthless transformation of all words into commodities," is a good case in point that discourse analysis and ideology critique are not at all mutually exclusive: F. Haug, "'Schaffen wir einen neuen Menschentyp': Von Henry Ford zu Peter Hartz," *Das Argument*, 252, 45, 4/5 (2003): 606–7.

53 Bröckling, "Totale Mobilmachung," 137.

54 Opitz "Gouvernementalität im Postfordismus," 102.

55 See O. Petersen, "Ausfaltung und Verfeinerung der Disziplinarmacht im Management – Erfahrungsbericht aus einer internationalen Unternehmensberatung," *Forum Kritische Psychologie* 47 (2004): 120–44.

56 Bröckling, "Totale Mobilmachung," 142.

57 Cf. the critique of Moldaschl's similar argument by I. Langemeyer, "Subjektivität und kollektive Erfahrung: Subjektivierung als Machtinstrument im Produktionsprozess," *Widerspruch: Beiträge zu sozialistischer Politik* 46, 24 (2004): 65–78.

58 A. Gramsci, *Selections from the Prison Notebooks of Antonio Gramsci*, ed. and trans. Q. Hoare and G. Nowell Smith (New York: International Publishers, 1971), 302, and *Quaderni del carcere*, 4 volumes, critical edn. by the Gramsci Institute, ed. V. Gerratana (Turin: Einaudi, 1975), Quaderni 4, §52, 489.

59 Bröckling, "Totale Mobilmachung," 144.

60 W. F. Haug, *High-Tech-Kapitalismus. Analysen zur Produktionsweise, Arbeit, Sexualität, Krieg und Hegemonie* (Hamburg: Argument-Verlag, 2003), 67.

61 J. Habermas, *Toward a Rational Society: Student Protest, Science, and Politics*, trans. J. J. Shapiro (Boston: Beacon Press, 1970 [1968]), 93.

62 Bröckling, "Totale Mobilmachung," 152.

63 Petersen, "Ausfaltung und Verfeinerung der Disziplinarmacht im Management," 141.

64 Opitz, "Gouvernementalität im Postfordismus," 141.

65 See I. Bakker and S. Gill, *Power and Resistance in the New World Order* (Houndsmill: Palgrave Macmillan, 2003), 192.

66 Opitz, *Gouvernementalität im Postfordismus*, 141.

67 Opitz, "Gouvernementalität im Postfordismus," 103.

68 See C. Müller, "Neoliberalismus als Selbstführung. Anmerkungen zu den 'Governmentality Studies,'" *Das Argument* 249, 45 (2003): 101–2.

69 See Bröckling, "Jeder könnte, aber nicht alle können," and Opitz, *Gouvernementalität im Postfordismus*, 103.

70 J. Butler, *The Psychic Life of Power: Theories in Subjection* (Stanford, CA: Stanford University Press, 1997), 17.

71 *Ibid.*, 111–12.

72 Cf. J. Rehmann, *Theories of Ideology: The Powers of Alienation and Subjection* (Chicago: Haymarket Books, 2014), 165–73.

73 Opitz, *Gouvernementalität im Postfordismus*, 84, 164–5.

74 *Ibid.*, 84.

75 Bröckling, Krasmann, and Lemke, eds., *Gouvernementalität der Gegenwart*, 13.

76 See A. Gramsci, *Selections from the Prison Notebooks of Antonio Gramsci*, 286, and *Quaderni del carcere*, Quaderni 1, §61, 72; Quaderni 22, §2, 2146.

77 Haug, *High-Tech-Kapitalismus*, 75–6.

78 See *Projekt Automation und Qualifikation (PAQ), Widersprüche der Automationsarbeit. Ein Handbuch* (Berlin: Argument-Verlag, 1987), 152ff., and Haug, " 'Schaffen wir einen neuen Menschentyp,' " 610–11.

79 B Ehrenreich, *Nickel and Dimed: On (Not) Getting By in America* (New York: Henry Holt & Company, 2002).

80 K. Marx, *Capital: A Critique of Political Economy*, vol. I, trans. B. Fowkes (London: Penguin Books, 1976), 793.

81 Bröckling "Totale Mobilmachung," 139.

82 See L. Wacquant, "Bourdieu, Foucault, and the Penal State in the Neoliberal Era," ch. 5 in this volume.

83 R. Castel, "From Dangerousness to Risk," in Burchell, Gordon, and Miller, eds., *The Foucault Effect*, 281–94.

84 P. Bourdieu et al., eds., *The Weight of the World: Social Suffering in Contemporary Society*, trans. P. Parkhurst Ferguson et al. (Stanford: Stanford University Press, 1999 [1993]), 63.

85 L. Wacquant, "Inside 'The Zone.' The Social Art of the Hustler in the American Ghetto," in Bourdieu et al., eds., *The Weight of the World*, 148 and n.9.

86 See Langemeyer, "Subjektivität und kollektive Erfahrung," 73.

7

Michel Foucault and the Spiritualization of Philosophy

Jean-Loup Amselle

The goal of the present chapter is to show how the thoughts of Michel Foucault fall within a movement of spiritualization of philosophy. Michel Foucault, along with Gilles Deleuze and Jacques Derrida, is one of those few French intellectuals and philosophers who have acquired a world-renowned reputation. Translated into several dozen languages, their works are considered to have renewed the social sciences and philosophy and are viewed as forces of challenge that call into question the established order. In particular, as I will try to show here, Foucault's thoughts, like those of Deleuze and Derrida – even if the latter only turned to Marxism at a late stage – manifest a rejection that is particularly relevant to dialectics and to historical materialism, and reveal, in reality, an eminently conservative character.

This aspect, which concerns his thought less than his position, is relatively difficult to grasp because he himself never officially broke away from Marxism, even if his work is entirely directed against this doctrine. Although he started his philosophical career before May 1968, it is in the upheavals of that revolution and their aftermath that the significance of his work really unfolds. And, therefore, his approach must be resituated with respect to the philosophers of the previous generation, in particular Jean-Paul Sartre, who similarly appeared to his successors to be the archetypal committed intellectual. Foucault, Deleuze, and Derrida, as well as Pierre Bourdieu, were effectively fascinated by the stature of the "total" intellectual of the author of *Being and Nothingness* and always positioned themselves with respect to him, even if, indeed, their philosophy represented a major rupture from his.

Sartre and the spiritualization of philosophy

If Sartre was what we would call a political companion of the French Communist Party (Parti Communiste Français, or PCF), this commitment was never made on behalf of or on the basis of Marxism, a doctrine that, in the end, he poorly understood. Moreover, in the postwar period, the more important works of Marx, *Capital* in particular, were largely ignored by FCP intellectuals and their allies. The latter oscillated between economism and dogmatism, and they referred primarily to Lenin and Stalin or refractory works in Soviet textbooks, rather than to the works of the founding fathers. We must be grateful to Althusser and his disciples for grappling with the task of reading this difficult work, even if they offered a structuralist interpretation largely inspired by Levi-Strauss and Lacan.

In short, Sartre shifted to the fringes of the proletariat, or away from his early vision, as he later became involved, under the influence of Fanon, with the "Wretched of the Earth," which is to say the peoples of the Third World, while always having an idealized concept of these people. His philosophy, associated with liberty, inter-subjectivity, and a phenomenological ontology inspired by Heidegger, was very far from an analysis in terms of productive forces, relations of production, and social formation. Thus, Sartre was used as a great intellectual figure by the PCF, as far as it suited this political party's interest, but this alliance was never made on an intellectual or philosophical basis, for the good reason that philosophy was in no way the PCF's central focus.

Sartre and Foucault

What is interesting to note about Sartre – and this is what connects him to Foucault – is that, despite the radical differences between these two thinkers, he was also, like Foucault, linked, albeit in different ways, to the Maoists of the Gauche prolétarienne (GP). Through the founding of the journal *Libération* in the early 1970s, Sartre created strong links with certain members of this small group – in particular with its leader Benny Levy, known by his alias Pierre Victor. It should also be noted that, even though the Union de la Jeunesse Communiste Marxiste-Léniniste (UJCML), ancestor of the GP, had not participated in the movement of May 1968, its heir played an important role in radicalizing after this period, without taking up arms as did the German Red Army Faction (RAF) and the Italian Red Brigades ("Brigate Rosse," BR). The renunciation of armed struggle also signified the renunciation of revolution and a search for new paradigms. As we know, a certain number of *soixante-huitards* abandoned all hope of radical societal change, and thus also abandoned commitment to collective groups (parties, organizations of all kinds) that had the intention of realizing this objective. They thus turned to solutions of individual salvation, notably to various religions – Catholicism, Islam, Judaism – that could represent, through their personal history and their affinities, an issue specific to their well-being. It is in this context that Benny Levy, the leader of the GP, carried out his "religious turn" by reconnecting to his family's religion and in becoming a kind of rabbi. When Sartre met Benny Levy, Sartre was old and physically diminished and was somewhat overwhelmed by Levy. The renewed faith of the leader of the GP spoke to the heart of an old philosopher searching for a new system of explanation for the world that could replace the old story of class struggle. It was thus natural that he adopted his young companion's religious view of the world.

Foucault vs. Sartre

The philosophy of Michel Foucault is very different from that of Sartre and, moreover, it was interpreted, when his first works appeared, as a radical change of paradigm. Foucault was part of the intellectual sphere marked by the structuralism of Levi-Strauss and Lacan in which the notion of "human liberty" no longer had a place. Priority was then given to a philosophy without subjectivity and dedicated entirely to analysis of mechanisms of power. What interested Foucault, through a broad historical investigation centered on the West, was to emphasize, parallel to economic phenomena, all the mechanisms of confinement that hold individuals in institutions like hospitals, schools, and prisons, and, as a result, the madman, the prisoner, and the homosexual held his attention even more than the proletarian class.

The research Foucault threw himself into, through his numerous works – too numerous to be an analyzed here in detail – aimed to update what he calls the "micro-physics of power," at the same time avoiding anything that concerned the state, and thus political philosophy. But this idea of micro-physics that applies to the bodies of individuals is in no way an instrument for enabling liberation. For Foucault, the idea of an emancipation of the proletariat that could lead to socialism and then to communism was thus very far removed from his thoughts. Indeed, he thought the opposite, I would say. Having attended some of his courses in the early 1970s, I remember the delight with which he spoke of the tortured bodies in public executions. Michel Foucault certainly did not hold power in contempt, but was rather, it seems to me, a philosopher who enjoyed power (not, of course, institutional power – he never directed a research center), but the idea of the power of surveillance, constraint, and punishment of the human body. So, do we have here Michel Foucault, S&M Philosopher? In any case, for Foucault, not only can there be no "sense of history" that we can attribute to him, but, in addition, there is also no movement of history, since nothing that is part of the Hegelian conceptual apparatus exists: not the dialectic of master and slave, the "negation of negation," or the ongoing confrontation between the dominant and the dominated.

It is via Heidegger, the deconstructor of Western metaphysics, that Foucault discovered Nietzsche. The reading of Nietzsche's works – notably *On the Genealogy of Morals* and *Thus Spoke Zarathustra* – is certainly a productive entry point into the thoughts of Foucault. The apology of slavery, the domination of the "blond beast," and the theory of the Übermensch, ideas that were sharply opposed to the Hegelian dialectic and to socialism, certainly had a strong influence on his approach.

In the period after May 1968, with the founding of Vincennes University, the ideas of Foucault and Deleuze triumphed. During these times, the author of *The Order of Things* maintained relatively close relations with the GP and, notably, Benny Levy. Foucault, denigrator of political philosophy, was essentially researching alternative models that would permit him to conceptualize power. Benny Levy's return to religion, which seduced Sartre, was also of interest to Foucault, who asked Levy to explain the model of the Pastor in the Hebraic literature.[1] In the Semitic pattern, as incarnated in Jerusalem, he sees a precursor of the reading of French history in terms of the "War of Two Races." The model of confrontation between the Franks from Germania and the indigenous Gauls, ancestors of the "Third Estate," offers a Nietzschean vision of history that allows Foucault to reject all ideas of a social contract, which, for him, is only a justification of the sovereignty of the state.[2]

On a more general level, Foucault uses every means necessary, avidly mobilizing all forms of knowledge that can call into question the ensemble of totalizing interpretations of history and society: not only political philosophy but psychology and Marxism as well. His principal enemy – the state, society, and the unconscious – is prone to confining the individual in an overall identification of some kind. Concerned with removing madmen, prisoners, and homosexuals from all forms of imprisonment and all unequivocal categorization, he is prepared to seize any theory – even the most reactionary, like neoliberalism and its unadulterated apology for the market – to render individuals their liberty and to allow them to escape all determinations emanating from society's apex.[3]

Similarly, Foucault sees in exotic thought, or the revolution of Iran's Mullahs, a radical way of ending the supremacy of Western philosophy, in which he joins the apostles of deconstruction such as Jacques Derrida, who, at the same time, relied on Arabic philosophy in order to carry out his Heideggerian project.

"Down with the Enlightenment." This could be the motto of the little philosophical world after 1968, this little world encompassing the Catholic and Gaullo-Leftist philosopher Maurice Clavel as well as the "new philosophers" André Glucksmann and Bernard-Henry Levy, to whom Foucault is close. They all took part in the fight against totalitarianism, for which they claimed Marxism was primarily responsible.[4]

What was called "La pensée 68" and "French Theory" are thus strongly marked by cultural studies and postmodernism. This signifies that cultural relativism was adopted by these thinkers, and that the very idea of total knowledge, to which Marxism aspired, was seen as an aberration. It is also in this way that the ideas of Foucault, Derrida, and Deleuze strongly influenced the great figures of postcolonialism, who progressively abandoned their Gramscian orientation in order to throw themselves into the arms of "French Theory."[5]

Michel Foucault and the spiritualization of philosophy

But the author of *Discipline and Punish* pursued another line, one that was concerned with spirituality. In *The History of Sexuality*, a broad historic–philosophical portrayal directed against psychoanalysis, Michel Foucault dedicates the third and final volume of this series to the theme of "ethical self-concern." In the last part of his life, Foucault, in ill health, in fact developed a philosophy of life close to the considerations of Pierre Hadot on the "spiritual exercises" of late antiquity, a philosophy itself closely inspired by the Stoics, Epicureans, and Cynics.[6]

Based notably on Plutarch, Seneca, and Epictetus, Foucault affirms that, following "a tradition that goes back a very long way in Greek culture, the care of the self is in close correlation with medical thought and practice."[7] According to Plutarch, for instance, philosophy and medicine belong to a single realm – that of *pathos* – which applies to the domain of passion, physical disease, disturbances of the body, and involuntary movements of the soul. Training and taking care of oneself are thus related activities, and Epictetus, who considers his school as a "clinic for the soul," wants his disciples to be more like patients than students.[8] Refusing to restrict the field of philosophy to its nineteenth-century university avatar, our two authors are willing to relocate it in a vaster domain that includes all the forms of wisdom developed in late antiquity, and notably the "spiritual exercises" which would subsequently undergo, in a different form, a powerful resurgence within Christianity. In the context of this new "spiritualist" understanding of philosophy, taken up by the general public in the numerous "philosophy cafés" and "popular universities," as well as in multiple interventions by philosophical media professionals like André Comte-Sponville, Michel Onfray and Luc Ferry, it becomes possible to establish a bridge between "concern for self" and "personal development." Without holding Pierre Hadot or Michel Foucault accountable in any way for this state of affairs, it's clear that the realignment of philosophy with the care that the subject must devote to itself, in both the spiritual and corporeal spheres, results in the isolation of the social milieu in which it evolves. In this sense, "spiritual exercises" and "concern for self," touted by Hadot and Foucault as Sufi mysticism and Shamanism, can be seen as extremely conservative techniques for psychological maintenance, in the sense that they refer individual expression or grievances back to individuals themselves, thus averting any condemnation of the society in which they live.[9]

All in all, Michel Foucault played a major role in the shift in thought – or the epistemic change, to use the conventional post-1968 vocabulary. Having eradicated all teleological narrative and ultimate goals from human history, Foucault was able to carry out an approach of "micro-narratives" focused on the modes of subjectivation of the individual throughout history. Although he is presented, along with Derrida and Deleuze, as being one of those who introduced "rebellious thought" into the modern world, his approach appears to me to be centered even more on a desperation symbolized by the watchwords "No Future."[10] The focus on "micropowers" that he initiated in fact consists of seeing power everywhere, and thus nowhere. In this sense, his position falls within a movement theorized by John Holloway, which aims to develop power niches in contemporary societies, along the lines of those created by the Zapatistas and subcomandante Marcos in the mountains of Chiapas, Mexico.[11] This is, in the true sense of the word, a revolution in revolution, in the sense that, for these movements, the question is no longer just one of controlling the state apparatus but one of developing zones of autonomy. This new political practice – which is sometimes derisively dismissed as "new age," as a result, for instance, of the subcomandante Marcos's obsession with extraterrestrials – closely tracks the declining activity of insurgents like the Revolutionary Armed Forces of Colombia (FARC) or the Shining Path Communist Party of Peru. It is no accident that the university and intellectual elite of Bogotá, Colombia, went, in just a few years, from Marxism to Shamanism, and that its members now consult shamans and consume hallucinogenic substances like Ayahuasca, rather than supporting guerillas.[12] The twenty-first century will be one of spirituality, and, in this sense, Michel Foucault foreshadowed the rise of vertical revolutions driven by identity, which have replaced class struggles. The priority is now on fragments rather than the totality, and Foucault – followed in this by Toni Negri with his notion of the "multitudes," and by Slavoj Žižek and Giorgio Agamben – will have become the proponent of political postmodernity. Even the Indignados movement in Spain and "Occupy Wall Street," which represent the acme of current political protest, are part of this change in paradigm, because they too are niches of autonomy and do not envisage the conquest of power. In passing from "revolution" to "indignation," in one fell swoop we both abandoned the desire to change the world and, as a consequence, installed ourselves in a space more conducive to communal living than the desire for insurrection.

This process of depoliticization reached its peak in France after the last presidential campaign and the compassionate "care" politics promoted by Martine Aubry, which echoes Foucault's idea of "ethical concern," and above all with the central role played by the think tank Terra Nova. While acknowledging the "decline" of the working class and its supposed betrayal in embracing the extreme right, the think tank's spokespersons played a determining role in the formulation of new watchwords that are likely to please the "ethno-eco-bobo" (bohemian-bourgeois) sections of the population targeted by the Parti Socialiste (PS). This strategy consisted – and still consists, despite a few hesitations by Hollande – of promoting austerity and lowering living standards for most people, in exchange for a few treats like "marriage for everyone," which are needed to help voters swallow the better medicine of social liberalism. But this policy of fragments, which is not applied to the Romani people (of Eastern Europe) in France or to the right of foreigners to vote in municipal elections, has yet to detract from the financial scandals of the PS's, leaders or Hollande's alignment with French business elites and German chancellor Angela Merkel.

The point, of course, is not to hold Foucault responsible for the Socialist Party's corruption after three years in power. Yet his thought did lead to the breakdown of the social realm into a myriad of singularities, which proved unable to coalesce into a force that could achieve emancipation for the many.

The struggle for the excluded of all kinds, for all the victims of various confinements, certainly represented something not considered by the Marxists, who are dedicated solely to the defense, or rather the representation, of the proletariat. It is true that the issues of gender, homosexuality, or prisons were not on the agenda of workers' parties, because the Revolution and the seizure of power were the only things that mattered to them, and they thus felt that only from this perspective – if it was possible at all – could the "secondary contradictions" be resolved. Michel Foucault had the great merit of drawing attention to these issues and of being responsible for a whole range of investigations, including those on gender.

On the one hand, this focus on fragments or singularities, while necessary, is not a politics; on the other hand, it harmonizes perfectly with neoliberalism and its leftist version, social liberalism.[13] How can we not see that the emphasis on singularities is fully consistent with new marketing strategies focused on the definition of niche markets?

Furthermore, if companies fear lawsuits brought against them for discrimination based on race or gender, they can also emphasize the affirmative action policy they implement in order to avoid wage increases.

Basically, the postmodern policy based on singularities, fragments, or multitudes could represent a form of adaption by capitalism to the new situation. By shifting the spotlight from the whole to fragments, neoliberalism, whether on the Right or the Left, has managed to "depoliticize" social actors is a way that has proved very useful for preserving the existing system. Under the cover of promoting and liberating various "societal" components, society and the state have made themselves vulnerable to an *aggiornamento*. Without consciously wanting to serve the interests of capitalism, Foucault and his followers have, in part, rendered obsolete old labor unions and political struggles based on wage claims and the conquest of the state. Through this strategy of dissemination and decline, symbolized in the economic realm by the designation of the individual as an "entrepreneur of the self" (Gary Becker) and in the field of philosophy as "ethical self-concern," each disruption of the social whole and each revolution will be provisionally placed on hold. Foucault will have thus harmoniously combined libertarian liberalism and personal development, in a "new age" philosophy that evicts social actors who see state and society as battlegrounds of the class struggle. What better gift to the market and those who benefit from it? How can we not realize that investors want only one thing, and that individuals are passive consumers of themselves?

Also, at the end of their lives, Sartre and Foucault, both great philosophers, performed an about-face in their thinking and turned to spirituality as their way of understanding the world. They certainly did it on different bases: Sartre from a spiritual view of Judaism acquired from Benny Levy, Foucault through an ancient spiritualism inspired by Pierre Hadot. While situated in totally opposed paradigms, one in intersubjectivity, the other in dehumanization – they found themselves, a few dozen years apart, communing in a kind of post-1968 faith. Indeed, only beginning in May 1968 did their thinking begin to converge. In fact, the explosion of French society at that time ultimately accomplished little – only a spiritual revolution. Without being transformed into a social and political revolution, May 1968 gave birth to a spiritual revolution, and it is in this state that we find ourselves today. The famous reduction of "social" to "societal" dates back to this failed revolution, and we are still paying for that failure to radically transform society.

Notes

1 For more on this subject, see J.-L. Amselle, *L'Occident décroché. Enquête sur les postcolonialismes* (Paris: Fayard/Pluriel, 2010), 42 n.2.

2 Cf. the chapter on "Michel Foucault et la guerre des races," in J.-L. Amselle, *Rétrovolutions. Essais sur les primitivismes contemporains* (Paris: Stock, 2010), 161–77.

3 M. Foucault, *The Birth of Biopolitics: Lectures at the Collège de France, 1978–1979*, trans. G. Burchell (London: Palgrave Macmillan, 2008).

4 See chapter 1 in this book by M. S. Christofferson.

5 On this point, see Amselle, *L'Occident décroché*.

6 P. Hadot, *Éloge de la philosophie antique* (Paris: Allia, 2003), and M. Foucault, *The History of Sexuality*, vol. III, *The Care of the Self*, trans. R. Hurley (New York: Pantheon, 1988), ch. 2.

7 Foucault, *The History of Sexuality*, vol. III, 54.

8 *Ibid.*, 55.

9 After rejecting Marxism – in his eyes, guilty of being compromised by Hegelian dialectics – and incensed by the Iranian revolution, Foucault, in the last phase of his life, performs a new and ultimate conservative turn-around.

10 "Foucault, Derrida, Deleuze, penseurs rebelles," *Sciences Humaines*, special issue (June, 2005).

11 On a recent book by *John Holloway*, see D. Bensaïd, available at libcom.org/book/export/html/35451.

12 On this subject, see Amselle, *Psychotropiques. La fièvre de l'ayahuasca en forêt amazonienne* (Paris: Albin Michel, 2013).

13 On this subject, see Nancy Frazer's interview "Féminisme et libéralisme ont entretenu des liaisons dangereuses," *Libération*, April 12, 2013.

8

The Great Rage of Facts

Michel Foucault[1]

Translated by Michael Scott Christofferson

What is the least insignificant thing that has happened in our heads in the last 15 years? I would say, in the first instance: a certain rage; an impatient, irritated sensitivity to what is happening; an intolerance for theoretical justifications and for all this slow work of pacification that the "true" discourse ensures from day to day. Against the backdrop of the thin scenery that philosophy, political economy, and so many other wonderful sciences have set up, the crazies have now risen up as well as the ill, the women, the children, the prisoners, the tortured, and the dead by millions. God knows, however, that we were all armed with theorems, with principles, and with words to crush all that. Whence the sudden thirst for seeing and hearing these strangers, so close? Whence the concern for these rude things? We have been seized by the great rage of facts. We have ceased to tolerate those who said to us – or rather the murmuring within us that said – "Little matter, a fact will never be anything by itself; listen, read, wait; it will be explained further along, later, above."

The age of Candide has returned, in which one can no longer listen to the universal little song that explains everything. The Candides of the twentieth century – who have traversed the old world as well as the new, through massacres, battles, mass graves, and terrorized people – exist. We have met them: Ukrainians, Chileans, Czechs, or Greeks. The moral goal of knowledge today is perhaps to make the real sharp, harsh, angular, unacceptable. Is it therefore irrational?

Most certainly, if to make it rational is to calm it down, to
fill it with a tranquil certainty, to put it through some grand
theoretical machine that produces dominant rationalities.
Most certainly, again, if to make it irrational is to make it
cease to be necessary and become something with which one
grapples, struggles, brawls – intelligible and attackable to the
very extent that one has "derationalized" it.

I recently heard Glucksmann say that one must abandon
Kant's old question: "For what may I hope?" He wanted us
to ask instead: "Of what must I despair?" What, in effect,
must one detach oneself from? What must one no longer allow
oneself to be lulled asleep or carried away by? What can one
no longer allow to go without saying, – that is, to say in our
stead and for us? Against the discourses that make us hold
still by the weight of their promises, Glucksmann has merrily
just written, laughing and screaming, a "treatise of despair."
The reference is a bit pedantic – please excuse me – and inap-
propriate. The role of the Kierkegaard of Marxism is much
coveted these days, and Glucksmann is not seeking it.

And yet his question well remains – as it does for every
philosopher of the last 150 years – how to no longer be
Hegelian. Except that Glucksmann does not ask how to turn
Hegel upside down, put him back on his feet, or on his head,
to lighten up his idealism, to give him weight with economics,
to fragment him, to humanize him. Rather he asks how to
not be Hegelian *at all.*

The decisive test for the philosophies of Antiquity was
their ability to produce sages; in the Middle Ages, to rationalize dogma; in the classical age, to ground science; in the
modern period, it is their skill in justifying massacres. The
first helped man to bear his own death; the most recent, to
accept the death of others.

For 150 years, the Napoleonic massacres had a heavy
posterity. But another type of holocaust appeared – Hitler,
Stalin (the intermediate phase between the two and the model
for the second is to be found undoubtedly in colonial geno-
cides). Now, an entire Left has sought to explain the gulag,
if not, like wars, by a theory of history, at least by the history
of theory. Massacres, yes, yes; but it was a terrible error.
Reread therefore Marx and Lenin, compare with Stalin, and
you will well see where the latter went wrong. So many

deaths, it is clear, could only come from a misreading. One could have predicted it: the Stalinism-error was one of the principal causes of this return to Marxism-truth that we witnessed in the 1960s. Against Stalin, do not listen to the victims; they would only have their torments to relate. Reread the theoreticians; they will tell you the verity of truth.

From Stalin, the frightened scholars go back up to Marx, as if climbing their tree. Glucksmann had the cheek to climb back down to Solzhenitsyn; that is the scandal of *The Cook and the Cannibal*.[2] But the scandal that was never pardoned was not that of placing the blame for future errors on Lenin or some other holy person; it was showing that there was no "error," that it remained wholly consistent, that Stalinism was the truth – "a little" stripped down, to be sure – of an entire political discourse, that of Marx and of perhaps others before him. With the gulag, one saw not the consequences of an unfortunate error, but the effects of the theories that were the "truest" in the realm of politics. Those who sought to escape by opposing the authentic beard of Marx to the false nose of Stalin did not like this at all.

The brilliance of *The Master Thinkers*, its beauty, its out-bursts, its enthusiasms, and its laughters, are not the product of temperament, but of necessity. Glucksmann wants to fight with his bare hands: not to refute one idea with another, not to put it in contradiction with itself, not even to raise factual objections to it, but to put it face to face with the reality that imitates it, put its nose in the blood that it condemns, absolves, and justifies. It is for him a matter of plastering onto ideas the death's-heads that resemble them. Everything has been done for so long so that philosophy can say, like Kaiser Wilhelm II inspecting the slaughterhouses of Verdun: "I had never wanted *that*." But Glucksmann pulls it by the sleeve, makes it descend from its dais, and makes it touch it with its own hands. And says – with a hint of brutality, I admit: "Go and say that you don't recognize yourself in this."

Recognize oneself in what? In the games of the state and of the revolution. The English Revolution of the seventeenth century had been prestigious. It served as an example; it dif-fused its principles; it had its historians and its jurists; in sum, it was valued essentially for its results. The French Revolu-tion, though, posed an entirely different set of problems, due less to its results than to the event itself. What had just happened? What did this revolution consist of? Is it *the* revolution? Can it, must it start again? If it is incomplete, must one finish it? If it is finished, what other history begins now? What must one henceforth do to make revolution, or to avoid it?

Once one scratches a little below the surface of the philosophers' discourses, but also below the political economy, history, and social sciences of the nineteenth century, what one finds is always the following: the constitution of knowledge about *the* revolution, for it or against it. What the nineteenth century had "to think," as the philosophers would say, is this great menace–promise, this already finished possibility, this uncertain return.

In France, it is the historians who interpreted the revolution, perhaps precisely because it belonged to our memory. History occupies for us the place of philosophy (French "philosophers" thought, certainly, like everyone, about revolution – they never interpreted it, except the two solitary figures who, the extreme opposites of each other, had such importance in their centuries: Comte and Sartre). From this, no doubt, comes the first concern of historians – with the remarkable exception of François Furet and Denis Richet[3] – to demonstrate above all else that the Revolution did indeed take place, that it is an unparalleled, locatable, and finished event. From this comes their zeal to place everything only in relationship to a revolution that, by its attractive force, "orders" all of the clashes, rebellions, and resistances that our society interminably experiences.

In Germany, the revolution was interpreted by philosophy. Not at all, according to Glucksmann, because lagging behind English political economy and French politics left the Germans only ideas for dreaming, but because they were, on the contrary, in an exemplary and prophetic situation. Successively crushed by the Peasants' War, the bloodletting of the Thirty Years War, and the Napoleonic invasions, Germany was in an apocalyptic state. It was the beginning of the world; the state must be born and the law begin. Germany had moved with the same desire toward the state and toward revolution (Bismarck, social democracy, Hitler, and Ulbricht easily stand in profile one after another); the fading away of the state and the postponement *sine die* of revolution have never been just passing fancies.

There, it seems to me, is the center of Glucksmann's book, the fundamental question that it poses – undoubtedly the first to do so: by what twist was German philosophy able to make revolution the promise of a real, of a good, state, and the state the serene and realized form of revolution? All of our submissiveness finds its principles in this double invitation: make the revolution quickly, and it will give you the state that you need; hurry to make the state, and it will generously dispense the reasonable effects of the revolution. Having to think about revolution, its onset and end, the German thinkers have pegged it to the state, and they have sketched the state-revolution with all its final solutions. Thus the master thinkers put together an entire mental apparatus, that which underlies the systems of domination and obedient behaviors in our modern societies. Still they had to ward off four enemies, four vagabonds, the questioners and the indifferent, who themselves refused, when confronted with the imminence of the state-revolution, to play the role of the horsemen of the apocalypse:

- The *Jew* because he represents the absence of soil, money that circulates, vagabondage, private interest, the immediate link with God, so many ways to escape from the state. Antisemitism, which was fundamental to nineteenth-century German thought, functioned as a long apology for the state. It was also the matrix of all the racisms that marked the mad, the abnormal, the aliens [*métèques*]. Do not be Jewish, be Greek, say the master thinkers. Know to say "we" when you think "I."
- Panurge the uncertain, because he always questions and never decides, because he wanted to get married and did not want to be a cuckold, because he sang the praises of infinite obligation. Enter instead into the Abbey of Thélème. There you will be free, but because one has ordered you to be. There you will do what you want, but the others will do it at the same time as you, and you with the others. Be obedient to the order to be free. Revolt: in so doing you will be within the law; not doing it, you will disobey, which is exactly what I tell you to do.
- Socrates, who knew nothing, but who foolishly drew from it the conclusion that the only thing he knew is that

he knew nothing. Whereas he should have prudently recognized: since I do not know, it is because others do. The conscience of ignorance must be a hierarchical conscience. Know, say the master thinkers, know, you the ignorant, that the savant knows in your place, as does the university professor, the graduate, the technician, the statesman, the bureaucrat, the party, the manager, the supervisor, the élite.

• Bardamu, finally, Bardamu the deserter, who said, the day when everyone was being skewered on bayonets, that all that was left was to "beat it."

Thus, the master thinkers teach, for the greater good of the state-revolution, love of the city, the obligation of law-abiding liberties, hierarchies of knowledge, acceptance of massacres without end. Glucksmann dismantles the pompous set that frames this great stage where, since 1789, with its entrances from the right and the left, politics is performed; and, in the middle of its scattered fragments, he tosses in the deserter, the ignorant, the indifferent, the vagabond. *The Master Thinkers* is, like some of the great books of philosophy (Wagner, Nietzsche), a history of theatre, where, on the same set two plays strangely mix together: *Danton's Death* and *Woyzeck*. Glucksmann does not invoke a new Dionysus under Apollo. He brings to light, at the heart of the loftiest philosophical discourse, these fugitives, these victims, these irreducibles, these continually disciplined dissidents – in short, these "bloody heads" and other pale forms that Hegel wanted to erase from Earth's night.

Notes

1 First published as M. Foucault, "La grande colère des faits," *Le Nouvel Observateur* 652 (May 9–15, 1977): 84–6. The translator thanks Nicole Rudolph for her many suggestions for improving the English-language text.
2 A. Glucksmann, *La cuisinière et le mangeur d'hommes. Essai sur les rapports entre l'État, le marxisme et les camps de concentration* (Paris: Seuil, 1975).
3 F. Furet and D. Richet, *La révolution française* (Paris: Fayard, 1965).

Conclusion: The Strange Failure (and Peculiar Success) of Foucault's Project

Michael C. Behrent

The French stand-up comedian Fernand Raynaud had a famous routine in the 1960s about a man who goes to see his tailor about a problem with a suit the latter had recently made for him. "Y'a comme un défaut," the timid customer explains – something seems wrong with it. One side is always falling off the shoulders – generally speaking, it doesn't fit well. The domineering tailor will have none of it. Your posture is wrong, he explains. Stand up straight, like a man. Raise your shoulders a bit. And hold your elbows like so. Soon, the customer finds himself walking out of his tailor's shop in a ridiculously contorted position – but with a suit that now fits him perfectly. How fortunate he is, he muses, to have found such a talented tailor – who can "pull off such a beautiful suit for a funny looking guy like me!" ("Réussir un si beau costume sur un type si mal foutu!")

In many ways, the contemporary reception of Foucault's late-1970s analysis of neoliberalism parallels the ironic narrative of Raynaud's sketch. In the great philosopher's account, "y'a comme des défauts" – something is not quite right. But Foucault's champions have been adroit at arguing that the suit is, in fact, a perfect fit – providing, that is, that we learn to wear it properly.

The first problem we notice is that Foucault delivered his lectures on neoliberalism in 1979, when this emergent economic paradigm was in its earliest, pioneering stages. The neoliberal mantras associated with Margaret Thatcher ("There is no alternative") and Ronald Reagan ("Government is not the solution to our problem; government is the problem") had yet to be uttered, just as the policies they would underwrite were several years away from being implemented (save for a few tentative first steps). The events that would truly mark the entry into the neoliberal age – NAFTA, the acceleration of European unification, the creation of the World Trade Organization – would not occur until at least a decade after Foucault's death. Yet this problem can be easily resolved if we bestow upon Foucault extraordinary prophetic powers, turning the "historian of the present" into a chronicler of things to come. Thus in a recent essay, Christian Laval, referring to a free-market initiative launched by French business interests in 2000 known as the *refondation sociale*, writes: "This reform, resting on 'entrepreneurial values' [and] seeking to make of the company a general model, is very precisely what twenty years earlier Michel Foucault had identified as neoliberalism's specific nature."[1] Once this adjustment is made, Foucault's 1979 analysis seems to fit contemporary neoliberalism rather more snugly.

Next, there is the nagging problem that much of what Foucault says about neoliberalism – particularly in the case of the German Federal Republic – is at best only indirectly related to what is commonly meant by "neoliberalism" at present – namely, the idea of "market fundamentalism." Thus, Laval, noting that Foucault correctly identified "the man of enterprise and production" as the target of neoliberal governmentality, remarks that Foucault, in making this point, draws on "two heterogeneous sources": Ordoliberalism's "policy of society," and Schutz and Becker's theory of human capital. He acknowledges, moreover, that this "connection, from the point of view of the history of ideas, is not at all self-evident."[2] Indeed, as is clear from an examination of the passage from the 1979 lectures that Laval is referencing, the Ordoliberals' emphasis on entrepreneurial society sought to promote a broad-based access to private property, "the encouragement of small farms in the countryside," the "development of ... non-proletarian industries, that is to say, craft industries and small business," and "the organic reconstruction of society on the basis of natural communities, families, and neighborhoods."[3] In short, while Foucault clearly believed that Ordoliberalism played an important role in the advent of a market-based political paradigm, he associates it with the aspirations of Europe's postwar leaders, particularly the conservative liberalism of Germany's Christian Democratic Union and its ideal of a "social market economy," far more than with the virulent strand of market fundamentalism that returned onto the scene in the 1970s and which has dominated the world order ever since. But if we can overlook this inconvenient fact, Foucault's account of neoliberalism fits to present circumstances very nicely.

A further difficulty lies in the fact that Foucault, for all of his emphasis on studying the practical dynamics of power, focuses, when considering neoliberalism, almost exclusively on texts (by Walter Eucken, Wilhelm Röpke, Friedrich Hayek, Gary Becker, and Adam Ferguson, to name a few). The question of the relationship between discourse and power in Foucault's thought, and the sense that he is prone to conflate them rather cavalierly, has often troubled his critics. Mitchell Dean, in chapter 4, speaks of Foucault's "concentration on the explicit neoliberal governmental rationalities and their objectives rather than technologies and their modes of implementation and the struggles that surround them."[4] Yet, faced with the fact that Foucault, in the 1979 lectures, dwells almost exclusively on programmatic statements and theoretical articles by economists (in contrast, say, to the prison-reform literature examined in *Discipline and Punish*, the prescriptive character of which is more explicit), sympathetic readers have made the case that Foucault saw neoliberalism less as a power technology than as a governmental "rationality." In *La nouvelle raison du monde*, an important attempt to propose a comprehensive account of neoliberalism using Foucauldian categories, Pierre Dardot and Christian Laval argue that "neoliberalism, before being an ideology or an economic policy, is first and foremost a *rationality*," noting that Foucault, in his course summary, described his "interpretation" of neoliberalism as "a possible level of analysis, that of 'governmental reason.'"[5] Yet such a theoretical justification of this approach allows one to nimbly sidestep the question of whether this "rationality" actually corresponds to how neoliberalism operates in practice. Hence the importance of Jan Rehmann's remark, in chapter 6, that "There is hardly any indication of the real place, relevance, and function of these highly ideological texts within the actual culture of enterprises, or in the general framework of neoliberal domination and its leadership methods."[6] Unless the discrepancy between these "rationalities" and really existing neoliberalism is acknowledged, an exclusive focus on discourse (even in the form of "guide-books") risks taking the claims of neoliberalism's advocates at face value (a danger that is, perhaps, exacerbated by Foucault's distaste for ideology critique, and, indeed, for the very concept of ideology). To avoid falling into this trap, Foucault's apologists must pretend that such tensions do not exist or can be easily dismissed.

Finally, there are Foucault's pronouncements in which he seems to look favorably on neoliberalism, or at least to be willing to endorse it tactically in the pursuit of his own battles. For instance, in his March 21, 1979 lecture, Foucault notoriously described American neoliberalism as far from being "exhaustively disciplinary," since it favored "an optimization of systems of difference" and a system in which "minority...practices are tolerated."[7] As Daniel Zamora reminds us in chapter 3, Foucault was critical of the French social security system in a way that harmonized with contemporary free-market critiques. In a 1983 interview, for instance, Foucault remarked: "our systems of social security impose a particular way of life to which individuals are subjected, and any person or group that, for one reason or another, will not or cannot embrace that way of life is marginalized by the very operation of the institutions."[8] Yet Foucault's apologists seek to downplay or even elide these pronouncements. In this spirit, Laval speaks of the "lasting confusions and errors" of analyses of Foucault that "pretend as if...neoliberalism is, for him, a form of emancipation from power, the advent of which he celebrated."[9] Once again, the real Foucault, the Foucault who speaks in the courses, has to be rearranged and adjusted to make his statements "fit" with what one would expect (or hope) him to say about the economic paradigm that defines our time.

The recent efforts to use Foucault's thought (specifically, but not exclusively, the 1979 lectures) depend, in short, on a kind of willing suspension of disbelief in what he actually said and the context in which he said it. The suit in which they would dress him – a prescient critique of contemporary neoliberalism – fits only insofar as we imagine Foucault in a somewhat improbable posture.

The chapters in this volume seek to provide a more plausible account of Foucault's political and intellectual positions in the late 1970s and early 1980s, and thus a more sober assessment of the theoretical possibilities of using his *oeuvre* to conceptualize the global neoliberal regime under which we now live. These parallel goals are reflected in the two methodologies adopted by the volume's authors: contextual intellectual history, on the one hand (Christofferson, Zamora, and my own contribution, and, somewhat more loosely, those of Dean and Amselle) and, on the other, that of critical social theory (Wacquant and Rehmann). Taken together, these essays can be seen as signaling the inadequacies of uncritical attempts to use Foucault's thought for understanding neoliberalism – or, in any case, for developing a theory of neoliberalism constructed on fundamentally Foucauldian principles. They provide, as it were, a series of warnings or precautions that scholars and perhaps even activists would be well advised to heed before seeking in Foucault everything they ever wanted to know about neoliberalism.

Specifically, the precautionary principles this volume's chapters put forth – a kind of prolegomena for any future (Foucauldian) theory of neoliberalism – can be distilled into the following claims:

- Foucault's theoretical attempts to address neoliberalism in the 1979 lectures occurred at the tail-end of a period in which Foucault had actively participated in the post-1968 Left's thoroughgoing critique of Marxism, communism, and the traditional Left's commitment to state-centered social change and revolution. This critique was opened on several overlapping fronts, including Solzhenitsyn's (re)exposure of the Soviet Union's "gulag archipelago," the *nouveaux philosophes'* attack on Marxism's latent totalitarianism, and the Second Left's challenge to "social statism" (as embodied in the common program of the Left). Foucault's interest in neoliberalism (as he understood it at the time) is best seen as participating in an effort to reinvigorate leftist politics with a new set of conceptual resources. (See Christofferson, Behrent, and Dean.)

- Foucault's interest in neoliberalism harmonized with his anti-statism, which was both theoretical (the belief that political theory must emancipate itself from its focus on the problem of sovereignty) and practical (his view that political action must encompass much broader goals than seeking transformation through control of the state). In chapter 1, Christofferson speaks, in this regard, of Foucault's "one-sided analysis of the state, which can do no good," noting not only that it is "too blunt an instrument to make sense of the twentieth century as it provides no means by which to distinguish between different regimes," but also that it left "Foucault vulnerable to [*nouveaux philosophe* André] Glucksmann's argumentation because he lacked the conceptual tools to effectively critique his simplifications." Foucault's problematic critique of the state would thus seem to account for his interest in free-market thought and his distinctly uncritical willingness to take it at its word. (See Christofferson, Behrent, Dean).

- Foucault's methodology and its philosophical underpinnings account (at least in part) for his attraction to neoliberalism, as well as the limitation of his analysis of the free-market creed. As I argue in chapter 2, Foucault's examination of neoliberalism in the 1979 lectures is closely linked to the Nietzschean conception of power he had developed over the course of the decade. Free-market liberalism "arises when power realizes that it has an interest *as* power in *limiting* power." Neoliberalism, in Foucault's conception, "has no need to hypothesize something *outside of* or *beyond* power, such as law, rights, or even liberty," since liberty, in his view, is neither a "metaphysical entity [n]or a human attribute", but merely "a side-effect of power – as [he] put it, "the independence of the governed in relation to the governing'."[10] Yet as Rehmann argues in chapter 6, Foucault's use of power – and, in particular, the slippery concept of governmentality – as the theoretical lens for examining neoliberalism proves singularly problematic. Specifically, Foucault's emphasis

on the productive dimensions of power in neoliberal governmentality – the way in which power elicits "self-
activation" from subjects – makes it possible to overlook
the rather glaring ways in which neoliberalism relies upon
overt forms of domination (i.e. what Foucault would call
power's negative dimension). Thus, according to Rehmann,
the governmentality studies that Foucault inspired overlook "the fact that neoliberal class-divides also translate
into different strategies of subjection: on the one hand
'positive' motivation, the social integration of different
milieus, manifold offers on the therapy-market, on the
other hand the build-up of a huge prison-system, surveillance and police-control," with the former "directed
toward the middle classes and some 'qualified' sections of
the working class," and "the latter mainly toward the
'dangerous classes.'" The focus on governmentality and
power, in other words, "obfuscate capitalist domination"
and blinds us to what Rehmann, quoting Marx, calls the
"despotism of capital" under neoliberalism.[11] Jean-Loup
Amselle's account of a tendency toward the "spiritualization" of philosophy in post-1968 is largely consonant
with this critique. (See Behrent, Rehmann, and Amselle).

• Finally, the chapters call attention to the evidentiary
shortcomings of Foucault's account of neoliberalism.
Scholars have been fact-checking Foucault's genealogies
for decades, but setting the record straight on neoliberalism is particularly important if we are to arrive at a lucid
understanding of our current economic situation. In
chapter 4, Dean lists a number of highly contested asser-
tions in Foucault's account of the emergence of neoliberal
governmentality, including his interpretation of Machiavelli and Smith's "invisible hand"; the omission of
Malthus; and the status of "order" in Ordoliberalism – to
name a few. And while Loïc Wacquant, in his essay, does
not specifically address Foucault's lectures on neoliberalism, he does nonetheless seek to correct Foucault's narrative regarding the history of modern penality. "In short,"
he argues,

> lacking a structural concept with which to anchor penality
> as a form of symbolic power accumulating in the higher

reaches of social space (what Bourdieu captures with the notion of "field of power"), Foucault misread the historical trend of modern Western penality when he prophesied the vanishing of the prison at the very moment it was entering a phase of rapid expansion and wholesale solidification.[12]

(See Dean and Wacquant.)

What then are we to make of Foucault's project, which has been incalculably influential in modern thought, in light of the patent shortcomings of his account of neoliberalism and his strategic attraction to the free-market creed? How is it that the man who is arguably the most discussed thinker of our era seems simultaneously essential and woefully inadequate to conceptualizing what is perhaps the critical issue of our age – the hegemony of globalized neoliberalism?

It seems perfectly possible that the ultimate reason for Foucault's failure to offer a convincing account of neoliberalism has much to do with the fact that his philosophical-political project has in many ways been immensely successful. Foucault famously described his task as writing a "history of the present." The "present" in question was, broadly speaking, post-World War II Western – and specifically European – society. As Western Europe emerged from the rubble of the "zero hour" of 1945 and struggled with how to manage the abandonment of its colonial empire, Europeans seemed at last to learn the lessons of their tormented history and to found a society based (however imperfectly) on political and social democracy. Speaking of this period, Tony Judt, who is perhaps the most distinguished historian of this period, writes: "as a modest substitute for the defunct ambitions of Europe's ideological past, there emerged belatedly – and largely by accident – the 'European model.' Born of an eclectic mix of Social Democratic legislation and the crab-like institutional extension of the European Community..., this was a distinctly 'European' way of regulating social intercourse."[13] The French economist Thomas Piketty notes, moreover, that during much of this period, France (like most other Western countries) became, economically speaking, significantly more egalitarian than it had been in the long nineteenth century: the share of national income held by the wealthiest 10 percent declined from 45–50 percent before World War I to 30–35 percent at present. The postwar decades that the French refer to as "les trente glorieuses" (the "thirty glorious years") were particularly important to this trend. Piketty writes:

> During the entire period of the *trente glorieuses*, during which the country, which was in the midst of rebuilding itself, experienced very strong economic growth (the strongest in the nation's history), France had a mixed economic system, a capitalism without capitalists, in a sense, or at least a state capitalism in which private property-owners had ceased to control the largest corporations.[14]

It was precisely during this period of "capitalism without capitalists" that Michel Foucault lived, and it was in this highly specific context that he contended that power, rather than class and economic domination, had become the crucial political question of the day. In many respects, Foucault's project – in its archeological as well as its genealogical moments – was aimed at exposing the repressive and normalizing forces lurking in the shadows of the emerging postwar "French" or "European" model: its psychiatric wards, its public health system, its humanistic discourse, its prisons – and, of course, its last-man-like confidence that, in matters of sexuality, it had invented happiness. When Duccio Trombadori asked Foucault how he had been led, after 1968, to refocus his interrogations on the question of power, Foucault explicitly invoked what he had learned from his experience living in various postwar European societies:

> What was the meaning of the profound malaise I felt in Swedish society [where he had lived from 1955 to 1958]? And the malaise I felt in Poland? [where he lived from 1958 to 1959]...What was in question everywhere? The manner in which power was exercised, not only the power of the state, but that which is exercised through other institutions or forms of constraint...In writing *Madness and Civilization* and *Birth of the Clinic*, I thought I was writing a genealogical history of knowledge. But the real guiding thread was the problem of power.[15]

The success of Foucault's critique of postwar society's latently repressive institutions has been real, as even a passing familiarity with social movements of the 1970s and beyond suggests. Antipsychiatry, feminism, and queer theory are only the most obvious movements that Foucault's thought brought to light and helped to conceptualize. The ultimate failure of Foucault's thought – despite its very tangible successes – may have less to do with the philosopher himself than with bad timing. Somewhat mischievously, Foucault saw neoliberalism, as it had begun to emerge in the 1970s, as sharing some of the anti-statism and cultural libertarianism that had informed his own critique of the postwar welfare state. In doing so, however, Foucault was fighting the last war. The massive restructuring of the European and, ultimately, the global economy was once again making relevant the very questions that Foucault believed had become relatively marginal to contemporary society – social class, economic equality, and "the despotism of capital." The tragedy of Foucault's thought is that the conceptual tools he had so skillfully deployed to shine a withering critical light on postwar society proved distinctly less trenchant when directed at the emerging neoliberal order – the contours of which, at the moment of his untimely death in 1984, Foucault could only have glimpsed in the vaguest of terms.

Notes

1 C. Laval, "L'entreprise comme nouvelle forme de gouvernement: usages et mésusages de Michel Foucault," in H. Oulc'hen, ed., *Usages de Foucault* (Paris: Presses universitaires de France, 2014), 146. I address the connection between the *refondation sociale* and Foucault via an analysis of the trajectory of Foucault's student François Ewald in M. C. Behrent, "Accidents happen: François Ewald, the 'antirevolutionary' Foucault, and the intellectual politics of the French welfare state," *Journal of Modern History* 82, 3 (2010): 585–624.

2 Laval, "L'entreprise comme nouvelle forme de gouvernement," 148–9.

3 M. Foucault, *The Birth of Biopolitics: Lectures at the Collège de France, 1978–1979*, trans. G. Burchell (London: Palgrave Macmillan, 2008 [2004]), 147–8.

4 M. Dean, "Foucault, Ewald, Neoliberalism and the Left," chapter 4, p. 97, in this volume.

5 P. Dardot and C. Laval, *La nouvelle raison du monde. Essai sur la société néolibérale* (Paris: La Découverte, 2009), 13–14. Foucault, *The Birth of Biopolitics*, 322.

6 J. Rehmann, "The Unfulfilled Promises of the Late Foucault and Foucauldian 'Governmentality Studies,'" chapter 6, p. 145, in this volume. Rehmann is specifically speaking of scholars who have been inspired by Foucault's approach, more than Foucault himself.

7 Foucault, *The Birth of Biopolitics*, 259–60.

8 See Zamora, "Foucault, the Excluded, and the Neoliberal Erosion of the State," chapter 3, p. 69, in this volume.

9 Laval, "L'entreprise comme nouvelle forme de gouvernement," 147.

10 M. C. Behrent, "Liberalism without Humanism: Michel Foucault and the Free-Market Creed, 1976–1979," chapter 2, pp. 32, 47, in this volume.

11 Rehmann, "The Unfulfilled Promises of the Late Foucault," pp. 144, 152.

12 L. Wacquant, "Bourdieu, Foucault, and the Penal State in the Neoliberal Era," chapter 5, p. 124, in this volume.

13 T. Judt, *Postwar: A History of Europe since 1945* (New York: Penguin, 2005), 7–8.

14 T. Piketty, *Le capital au XXIe siècle* (Paris: Seuil, 2013), 428, 219–20.

15 Foucault, "Entretien avec Michel Foucault," interview with D. Trombadori (1980), in *Dits et écrits*, vol. IV, *1980–1988*, ed. D. Defert, F. Ewald, and J. Lagrange (Paris: Gallimard, 1994), 82.

Index